EARLY AMERICAN INTEREST IN VEDANTA

EARLY AMERICAN INTEREST IN VEDANTA

Pre-Emersonian Interest in Vedic Literature and Vedantic Philosophy

J. P. RAO RAYAPATI

ASIA PUBLISHING HOUSE, INC. New York

Library of Congress Catalog Card No: 72-87302

ISBN 0-210-40508-2

Printed in the United States of America

To
PRASHANT and ANAND

ACKNOWLEDGEMENTS

I THANK the reference librarians at the Library of Congress, American Philosophical Society Library, Library Company of Philadelphia, and New York Public Library for their cooperation and help.

My grateful thanks go to the Board of World Missions of the Lutheran Church in America for a research grant in preparing this book.

For instilling a scholarly discipline in me, through direction and example, I owe my deepest thanks to Dr. Hennig Cohen and Dr. Theodore Hornberger of the University of Pennsylvania.

J. P. RAO RAYAPATI

PREFACE

LITERATURE contains philosophy. This is especially true of ancient literature, which usually provides the foundations for philosophical and religious speculation. Thus Vedic literature, which began to be composed as early as 1500 B.C., has become the scripture of India. It is also the basis of many religious doctrines, philosophical systems, and popular cults even of modern India. The most attractive system to emerge from Vedic literature is Vedantic philosophy which is essentially monistic. Its attraction is the universal appeal of its idealism and optimism, its synthesis of rationalism and mysticism, and of pragmatism and spiritualism.

The oldest literature central to the life and culture of Colonial America is the Bible. Like Vedic literature, Biblical literature contains foundations for more than one system of theology and philosophy. Some of its most influential ideas are also monistic and spiritualistic. Thus, in spite of Puritan vigilance, monistic Christian ideas caused Puritan divines like Edward Taylor and Jonathan Edwards to express monistic idealism and an all-embracing spirituality. Every now and then monistic Christian ideas also caused a Quaker like John Woolman, or an explorer like William Bartram, to recognize the oneness and, therefore, the sacredness of all forms of life. Towards the end of the eighteenth century, America was ready to recognize the parallels that exist between native American idealism and alien Vedantic idealism.

In examining the exact process of exchange of these ideas in early America, one must avoid broad terms like "Orientalism" and "Asiatic," now obsolete as a result of comparative studies of philosophy, literature, and civilization. The following study will therefore deal with early American interest in the specific field of Vedic literature and Vedantic philosophy. Unfortunately, there has even been some confusion about terms in Vedantic philosophy — such as *Brahman, Ātman, Māya,* and *avidya.* It is necessary to define those terms and indicate their technical denotations within the system of Vedantic philosophy. For the sake of accuracy, one should fix the spellings of *Brahman, Brahma, Brāhmana,* and *Brahmin* in relation to their precise meaning. Except in quotations, I spell Sanskrit words in the phonetic script that is now used by modern American Sanskrit scholars.

In addition, I hope to blast the myth that Hindu thought is essentially pessimistic and other-worldly. I hope this will contribute to a ready recognition of the affinities that American transcendentalism has with Vedantic philosophy. While maintaining some measure of accuracy in the use of Vedantic terms, I have taken the liberty to define "Vedic literature" as all Sanskrit literature that was available to American readers prior to 1840. The term "Vedic literature" is an invention caused by necessity. I needed to find a term that would include all the English, Latin, French, and German translations of Sanskrit literature that were "discovered" unsystematically and at random up to 1840.

There have been several specialized studies of American transcendentalism. O. B. Frothingham's book, *Transcendentalism in New England* (Boston, 1876), argues for its development from indigenous ingredients. Frederic I. Carpenter's *Emerson and Asia* (Cambridge, Mass., 1930) summarizes Emerson's interest in a romantic "mythical Asia." Arthur Christy's *The Orient in American Transcendentalism* (New York, 1932) concerns itself with Emerson, Thoreau, and Alcott and their broad interest in "the Orient." V. K. Chari's *Whitman in the Light of Vedantic Mysticism* (Lincoln, Nebr., 1964) interprets Whitman's philosophy without investigating the derivation of Vedantic ideas from Vedic literature. No scholar has described the Vedic literature which was available to American readers prior to Emerson, Thoreau, and Whitman. How much was known of this Vedic literature, how early, and in what form it was presented to early American readers, are the subjects of this investigation. I have supplied a check-list of Vedic books in translation that were available in America prior to 1840 in order to suggest their popularity and to support the general argument of this book.

Described here, are the pioneering English translations of Sanskrit by British scholars — Sir William Jones, Charles Wilkins, H. T. Colebrooke, and H. H. Wilson; the efforts of

French Sanskrit scholars — Duperron, Langlois, and the Abbé Dubois; the concurrent work of German scholars — Christian Lassen, and T. A. Rixner, and the almost immediate response of historians of ancient philosophy — Degerando, Heinrich Ritter, and Udolph Wagner. Also described here are the English translations and critical estimates of Vedanta by Christian Missionaries — Carey, Ward, and Marshman. So is the rise of reformist fervor in the person of Rammohan Roy and the favorable results in the form of his reinterpretations of Vedantic "monotheism." Even the accounts of some travelers and historians of British India are included. These were the channels by which Vedic literature and Vedantic philosophy were made available. Some of this literature was discussed in the early American periodicals. The most sophisticated discussion was conducted in the New York *Commercial Advertiser, The North American Review,* and *The Christian Register.* The present study is an attempt, then, to assess the significance of this early American discussion of Vedic literature and Vedantic philosophy.

Early American interest in the literary and philosophical heritage of India is important in that it indicates a slow development of a favorable American response to Vedic literature. Prior to the actual translations of Vedic literary sources, American eclecticism meant the acceptance of European literary heritage. But after the availability of Vedic literature in English and European translations, American eclecticism took a sharp turn towards philosophies beyond Europe. This turn is most clearly indicated by the publication of *The Dial* in 1840. After 1840, Emerson, Thoreau, and (to some extent) Whitman, implicitly looked to Vedic literature as an important contribution to the total human heritage. Therefore, throughout this dissertation, "early American" interest means the pre-1840 American interest in Vedic literature and Vedantic philosophy.

The results of the present study indicate that Vedic literature was read in early America mainly out of an interest in the curious. There are occasional indications that reviewers were impressed by Vedantic ideas summarized in some accounts. The fact that Vedantic philosophy is a highly systematic philosophy with a complicated metaphysics did not seem to occur to any of the early American readers.

Emerson, Thoreau, and Whitman have been chosen for special

consideration in this study, because they are the chief exponents of transcendentalism and the most distinguished literary figures of the Transcendental period in American literature. Even their interests in Vedic literature and Vedantic philosophy prior to 1840 have been treated under the category of "early American interest." Their subsequent interest in Vedic literature and Vedantic philosophy has not been taken into account here because this area has been explored in scholarly articles and dissertations readily accessible. The most remarkable feature about the chief American transcendentalists is that their eclecticism is both literary and philosophical. Our world needs their outlook.

J. P. RAO RAYAPATI

CONTENTS

Preface   *vii*

Acknowledgements   *xi*

1. VEDANTIC PHILOSOPHY IN AMERICAN TRANSCENDENTALISM   1

2. SOME VEDANTIC TENDENCIES IN THE RELIGIOUS HERITAGE OF AMERICA   24

3. EARLY AMERICAN INTEREST IN THE LIFE AND WORKS OF SIR WILLIAM JONES   37

4. OTHER WORKS ON VEDIC LITERATURE AND VEDANTIC PHILOSOPHY AVAILABLE IN AMERICA BEFORE 1840   61

5. EARLY AMERICAN DISCUSSION OF VEDIC LITERATURE AND VEDANTIC PHILOSOPHY   80

6. CONCLUSION: EARLY VEDIC READINGS BY AMERICAN TRANSCENDENTALISTS   93

Appendix   107

Selected Bibliography   121

Index   131

1

VEDANTIC PHILOSOPHY IN AMERICAN TRANSCENDENTALISM

A REVIEW of existing literary-historical scholarship on the indebtedness of American transcendentalists to Vedic literature and Vedantic philosophy leaves us in utter consternation. Much of it is a scrupulous documentation of the "Oriental" reading of the transcendentalists. It is often accompanied by speculation about the kinship of ideas between American transcendentalism and Vedantic philosophy. One also notices a considerable misinterpretation of Vedantic concepts and terminology.

Vedic literature and Vedantic philosophy reached American readers as early as the last decade of the eighteenth century but its early history in America has not been adequately described. Within half a century American interest in Vedic literature and ideas gradually intensified. This interest culminated in Ralph Waldo Emerson's eclecticism when he, with the help of Henry David Thoreau, published selected translations of Vishnu Sarma's *Hitopadeśa,* and Manu's *Manavadharmaśaśtra* in *The Dial* of July, 1842 and January, 1843.[1] There are many questions left unanswered. What were the earliest translations of Vedic literature that were available in America? When did they reach America? Who were the first readers of Vedic literature? What were the Vedantic ideas those early readers confronted in their reading? To what extent did those readers understand Vedantic ideas? Did they accept any of those ideas? Or did they confront and reject them? What shifts did those ideas cause in the intellectual climate of the times? How did the early American readers of Vedic literature come to know about the early Sanskritists? How popular were the accounts of the lives and achievements of the early Sanskritists? Answers to these questions would help explain the

[1] Pp. 82-85; pp. 331-340.

gradual process of the growth of American interest in Vedic literature and Vedantic philosophy.

The present study is an attempt to establish the proper place
of Vedic literature and its ideas in the development of American
transcendentalism and also to clarify the definitions of some of
the important Vedantic terms and concepts. To begin at the beginning, it presents an account of the lives of the Sanskritists; it
then traces their popularity in America, and the slow but steady
development of American familiarity with Vedic literature and
Vedantic philosophy.

In various lands during different epochs, the search for truth
assumes different forms. Among those lands one finds occasional
reciprocal exchanges. But the best thinkers always assimilate and
digest these exchanges. They even convert them to their own forms
of thinking. Sometimes the assimilation is the result of a close resemblance in their respective ideas. Megasthanes, who around
315 B.C. was perhaps the first cultured Greek to live for a lengthy
period in India, was perceptive of the parallels between Indian
and Greek philosophies. "In many points," he wrote, "their teaching agrees with that of the Greeks—for instance, that the world
has a beginning and an end in time, that its shape is spherical,
that Deity, who is its Governor and Maker, interpenetrates the
whole.... About generation and the soul, their teaching shows
parallels to the Greek doctrines, and on many other matters. Like
Plato, too, they interweave fables about the other world and so
on."[2] This, for instance, was how a learned Greek grasped the
bare essentials of Indian thought that gave rise to systematic philosophies some centuries later. Here are two peoples discovering
the parallels in each other's forms of thinking and beginning to
sympathize with and understand each other's thought nearly three
centuries before Christ.[3]

Like Megasthanes, Emerson, Thoreau, and Whitman discovered Indian thought and recognized the parallels it has with their
own. They exulted over their discovery. Megasthanes noticed only
parallels between Indian and Greek thought. This is to say that
similar patterns of thought developed in independent sets of circumstances. Therefore, we should also consider whatever parallel
circumstances there are that can be traced in the early literary-

[2] George Woodcock, *The Greeks in India* (London, 1966), p. 149.
[3] E. J. Rapson, *The Cambridge History of India* (Bombay, 1962), p. 149.

philosophical history of India and America which influenced the rise of transcendentalism, for transcendentalism does not always derive from external literary-philosophical exchanges alone. In America, too, there were several independent tendencies and we should recognize them as the possible sources of transcendental tradition. But we shall limit ourselves only to those circumstances and independent tendencies in America which parallel the rise of transcendental thought in the literary-philosophical history of India.

Scholars have already made some critical estimates of the influence of Indian thought and literature on Emerson and his fellow transcendentalists. As early as 1930 Frederic Ives Carpenter, in *Emerson and Asia,*[4] concluded that Emerson approached Asia, not as a land of specific geographic boundaries, but as a land of mystery. "It was [for Emerson] a symbol for the unknown—for the other half of the world—for mystery, and romance, and poetry, and love, and religion."[5] In these words Carpenter described how Emerson transformed Asia into a romantic myth. He also pointed out that "One of Emerson's names for Lydian Emerson, his wife, was 'Mine Asia.' "[6] And he went on to ask these rhetorical questions: "Was she not also mysterious and fascinating to him? Did she not also belong to the other half of the world?—East and West, Asia and Europe, Woman and Man, the feminine and the masculine principles—were they not all names for the same two poles of Nature—the same two elements of life?"[7] These questions illustrate Carpenter's own mythical idea of Asia which, he insisted, was also Emerson's. Throughout his book he maintained certain stereotyped myths about an imaginary dichotomy between Asia and Europe, between the Orient and the Occident. He elaborated the stereotypes thus: "In general Asia is feminine, the passive, the religious, the contemplative, 'the ocean of love and power;' while Europe is the active, the practical, the definite, the inventive."[8] Again, he went on, "The Oriental mind was not troubled by practical details and minutiae. It cared only for the elemental things."[9] It is possible that Emerson held such views about Asia. In fact, Carpenter offered so much evidence from Emerson's *Journal,* and essays, and poems, that the reader cannot help but

---

[4] (Cambridge, Mass., 1930); hereafter cited as Carpenter.
[5] *Ibid.,* p. ix.   [6] *Ibid.,* p. 30.   [7] *Ibid.,* pp. 30-31. [8] *Ibid.,* p. 32.
[9] *Ibid.,* p. 33.

agree that Emerson really thought of Asia as one half in a dichotomous human nature of which Europe is the other half. But Emerson did not accept such myths consistently as we shall see in the final chapter of the present study. Moreover, Carpenter's opinion that the Oriental mind did not care for "practical details and minutiae" falls short of an adequate understanding of the "Oriental mind." The Hindu Grammarian Panini, for example, has been regarded by historians of linguistics as a mastermind in the detailed analysis of the phonemic and syntactical structure of Sanskrit.[10] Panini lived in the "second half of the fourth century B.C."[11] Even then, Panini must have been only the culmination of a long tradition of linguistic analysis throughout the Vedic age, i.e. up to 450 B.C.[12]

Such special care for "practical details and minutiae" as exemplified by Panini's grammatical studies antedates,[13] by at least a few centuries, Greek or Roman or European or "Western" concern for "details and minutiae" as Carpenter called them. In China, Confucian thought has initiated practical-mindedness. Similar claims can be made in favor of Israel which also is a very important Asian country. In Israel great care for "practical details and minutiae" became such a religious obsession that it helped preserve much of the ancient learning of Asia. In other words, Asiatic care for "practical details and minutiae" has given the modern world much of its existing scripture. It seems simplistic that Carpenter should have thought that "The Oriental mind was not troubled by practical details and minutiae."

Carpenter's "Asia" is not only mythical but it excludes much important information about Asia's intellectual character. He also excluded, for instance, the Bible from the literature of the Orient. Thus, he is thoroughly misleading when he said: "The Bible has been the book of Christianity, and Christianity has been the re-

---

[10] John T. Waterman, *Perspectives in Linguistics* (Chicago, 1963), p. 3.

[11] Theodor Goldstücker, *Panini: His Place in Sanskrit Literature* (Varanasi, India, 1965), p. 91. Also see Hajme Nakamura's *Ways of Thinking of Eastern Peoples, India, China, Tibet and Japan* (Honolulu, 1964), pp. 13, 14, 17; hereafter cited as Nakamura.

[12] Mauriz Winternitz, *A History of Indian Literature,* translated into English by Mrs. S. Ketkar (Calcutta, 1959), p. 3; hereafter cited as Winternitz.

[13] John T. Waterman, *Perspectives in Linguistics* (Chicago, 1963), p. 3; also Nakamura, pp. 13-17.

ligion of the Occident; and so, for all Westerners and for Emerson, the Bible has formed a part of Occidental literature."[14] The Bible, even of the Christian canon, consists of writings which are outright products of the so-called "Asian mind." On matters of imagery, concepts, and mysticism, major portions of the Christian Bible, not the least of which are the Gospels, are Asian. Indeed, Emerson, Thoreau, and Whitman understood very well the Asian nature of the mind and thought of the Bible. The Bible led them to take a deeper interest in the rest of the literatures of Asia and its intellectual heritage.

Today, terms like "Asian mind," "Oriental character," and "Eastern ways of thinking" have lost their meaning because of comparative studies of literature, philosophy, religion, sociology and science. Most early European scholars of "Oriental" studies, however, contrasted East with West. Emerson himself probably was a victim of such approach on occasions. But Carpenter's world has vanished. His "Asia" and his "Oriental mind" do not exist today.   ,

A Japanese scholar and philosopher Hajme Nakamura attacks this myth of East versus West in the following words:

In the four and a half centuries from the European 'discovery' of Asia to the present period of intensified culture contact, Europeans and Asians alike have learned all too little about each other. False antitheses and monolithic comparisons have persisted. . . .[15]

Besides, there has been a tremendous amount of diversity of thought and culture both in the East and the West, and Nakamura points out this diversity in the following words:

There has long been a tendency to think in terms of a dichotomy between East and West, presupposing two mutually opposed cultural sets of values labelled 'Occidental' and 'Oriental.' Thus the Oriental way of thinking is represented as 'spiritual,' 'introverted,' 'synthetic,' and 'subjective,' while the Occidental is represented as 'materialistic,' 'extroverted,' 'analytic,' and 'objective.' This sort of explanation of paired opposites is now rejected as too simple, the cultures of the 'Orient' and 'Occi-

[14] Carpenter, p. ix.   [15] Nakamura, p. v.

dent' are too diversified and each one is extremely complex.[16]

He goes on to indicate the diversity within the so-called Western heritage:

> . . . the Greek and the Hebrew civilizations, among the historical components of Western civilizations, differ markedly from each other. Moreover, the civilization formed by the fusion of these strains is divisible into the ancient, medieval, and modern periods, each of which has its peculiar characteristics; and further, modern Western civilization takes on different characteristics from nation to nation.[17]

Carpenter's understanding of Vedanta and his interpretation of Vedanta in Emerson's thought suffered from many misconceptions. For example, his treatment of Fate in Emerson's thought will suffice. Explaining Fate, Carpenter wrote, "The Hindus had said in effect: the deeds of earlier men whose souls have migrated into the bodies of men of later generation have affected these later men, by increase or decrease of the vital force transmitted."[18] Such a statement is a thorough misrepresentation of the Vedantic concept of Fate. The youthful Emerson, it is true, was led to believe that Fate in India ". . . is the dread reality, it is the cropping out in our planted garden of the core of the world; it is the abysmal Force, untameable and immense."[19] But Emerson outgrew this view. In the light of our present knowledge of Vedanta, his definition appears to be a matter of speculation and interpretation based on hearsay. Indeed, in India too, many privileged people offered such an "untameable" interpretation of Fate in order to justify the institution of caste and its hierarchical social structure. It also permitted the privileged castes to stand clear of social responsibility. But in Vedic literature and Vedantic philosophy, Fate is the law of *Karma,* or merely compensation. Emerson's own ideas on compensation are closer to the *Upaniṣadic* ideas of Fate or Karma than to subsequent interpretations of it, both in India and abroad, as "dread reality, the abysmal force, untameable and im-

---

[16] *Ibid.*, p. 3.   [17] *Ibid.*, p. 4.   [18] *Carpenter*, pp. 142-143.

[19] Ralph Waldo Emerson, *Journals,* ed. Edward Waldo Emerson, *et al.* (Boston, 1903-1912), Vol. VII, p. 123; hereafter cited as Emerson, *Journals.*

mense." But to Emerson as to the anonymous teachers of the
Upaniṣads, Fate is the operation of a natural law, a law of returns
or compensation, or a law of conservation of matter and actions
of the individual. In the light of the above remarks, it becomes
clear that we need a fresh approach both to a treatment of Vedanta
and to an application of the Vedantic system of ideas to Emerson's
thought.

In fact, Carpenter does not seem to have been aware of
Vedanta as a system of philosophy. Only once does the term
Vedanta appear in his book and, then, it is in a passage quoted
from Emerson's *Journal*.[20] What Carpenter achieved was a
complete documentation of Emerson's reading in the then available literature from India, Persia, and China which to him
constituted "Asia." This heavy reliance on Emerson's reading
naturally led him also to document his subject's opinions on the
literature and philosophies of "Asia" without making distinctions
between the youthful Emerson's meagre understanding and the
mature Emerson's informed appreciation. Carpenter also failed
to distinguish among the various philosophies of "Asia" as well
as between philosophies and mythologies, or folk-lore. This is
seen in the chapter he devoted to Emerson's interest in India
to which he gave the spurious title, "The Wisdom of the
Brahmins,"[21] a title as ambiguous as the title of his book.
"Wisdom" could mean philosophies or mythologies, which are
often contradictory. Brahmins certainly have sought to preserve
the wisdom of India. But they are not the sole originators of or
contributors to India's wisdom.

If, by "The Wisdom of the Brahmins," Carpenter meant
Vedanta, then he was misinformed. Vedanta, as the philosophy
of the *Upaniṣads*, is the product not only of the Brahmins but also
of the Kṣatriyas, the soldier class. Particularly, the doctrine of
transmigration and oneness of spirit seems to have been propound-
ed by Kings of the Kṣatriya caste. Mauriz Winternitz points
out the non-brahmanical origins of Vedanta in unmistakable
terms:

In the Upaniṣads, however, we are repeatedly told that kings
or warriors are in possession of the highest knowledge, and,
that the Brahman [a variant for Brahmin] Gautama, father of

[20] Carpenter, p. 145.   [21] *Ibid.,* pp. 103-158.

Śvetaketu, goes to king Pravahana in order to be instructed by him concerning the Beyond . . . . the king does impart the doctrine to him,—and it is the doctrine of *transmigration,* which here, where for the first time it appears clearly and distinctly, proves to be a doctrine which emanated from the warrior-class, and was originally foreign to Brahmanical theology.[22]

Another passage proves that the chief doctrine of the *Upaniṣads,* too, the doctrine of the *Atman,* the All-One, originated in non-brahmanical circles.[23]

Therefore it is inaccurate from the above historical perspective, to refer to the philosophy of the *Upaniṣads,* that is, Vedanta, as "The Wisdom of the Brahmins," and it becomes imperative to revise the terminology used by Carpenter.

At this point we should also fix the meanings of certain terms with a view to keeping certain distinctions of meaning and usage in our mind. The term *brahmin* is the Anglicized form of Sanskrit *brahmaṇa,* meaning a member of the sacerdotal caste of India. *Brahmanical literature* is the collection of works called *Brahmaṇas* which form part of Vedic literature. The Brahmaṇas were appended to the Vedas and chronologically they are pre-Upaniṣadic in composition. They consist of several magical prayers said to have an inherent power of their own. They are of interest especially to the student of religion who wishes to investigate the role of sacerdotalism in manipulating power-beliefs. They have probably exaggerated the exclusive identity of the Brahmins and forever put them at the top of the caste hierarchy. For this reason, the term *brahminism* connotes a tradition of exclusiveness.[24] Therefore, it is not accurate to refer to the Vedantic ideas of Emerson as *Brahmanism.* Emerson did not uphold sacerdotal exclusivism. In fact, he relinquished his orders as a minister. Part of the reason is that he was in favor of the idea of universal priesthood.

Following the example of Carpenter, Leyla Goren has written an interesting book which perpetuates all the myths discussed above. She characterizes Emerson as a mystic, longing for union

[22] Winternitz, p. 201. Also see *Kauṣitaki Upaniṣad,* I, i, where the Kṣatriya Citra instructs the first of the priests, Aruni, about the Beyond.
[23] *Loc. cit.;* also see *Chandogya Upaniṣad,* V, ii.
[24] Webster's *New International Dictionary,* 3rd edn.

with "God," just as the Brahmins of ancient India have done. She quotes from the *Upaniṣads* to elucidate the mystic content of Vedanta. But, unfortunately, she calls her little book *Elements of Brahmanism in the Transcendentalism of Emerson*.[25] Here is another instance of the misuse of the term *Brahmanism*. Her use of this term is especially inaccurate because she has quoted only from the *Upaniṣads* and never once from any of the *Brahmaṇas*.

Brahman is another term frequently occurring in Vedanta and very frequently misunderstood. It is spelled with an 'a' in the final syllable in order to distinguish it from Brahmin, the priest. *Brahman* is the term for the Ultimate Reality and the Absolute Spirit. The concept of *Brahman* is discussed in a later part of this chapter in connection with an exposition of the Vedantic worldview. For the present it is enough to know that *Brahman* is spirit, *Brahmin* is the priest, and that *Brahminism* is a sacerdotal tradition derived from the literature of *Brahmaṇas* which like the *Upaniṣads* are appended to the Vedas.

Carpenter discussed Buddhism and Emerson's attitude towards it in the chapter on "The Wisdom of the Brahmins," which suggests that he thought Buddhism an integral part of "Brahminism." There is no doubt today that Buddhism has its origins in some of the teachings of the *Upaniṣads*. But in relation to Hinduism, and particularly to "Brahminism," its position is like that of the New Testament to the Old.[26] Buddhism is a departure from Brahminism.

Two years after Carpenter's book appeared Arthur Christy published *The Orient in American Transcendentalism*.[27] His research in the history of ideas of India, Persia, and China was extensive and accurate. His expository method includes more than a mere documentation of the "Oriental" reading of his subjects. But the title and the claims of the title are somewhat misleading. The title promised a study of "the Orient" in *American* transcendentalism, but the subtitle informs us that his book is "a study of Emerson, Thoreau, and Alcott." His achievement in the book was great, but his coverage was not really representative of *American* transcendentalism. He ignored Walt Whitman and the Quaker heritage of America that led to the rise of transcendentalism. He missed an account of American discussion of the earliest English transla-

---

[25] (New York, 1959), pp. 31-60, reprinted in *ESQ* (1964), First Quarter.
[26] Winternitz, p. 45.
[27] (New York, 1932); hereafter cited as Christy.

tions of Vedic literature. He seems to have regarded transcendentalism as a New England monopoly. At one point he referred to it as "the composite Orientalism of Concord."[28] Regardless of the reason for omitting Whitman in his anthology, *The American Transcendentalists: Their Prose and Their Poetry,* Perry Miller acknowledged Whitman as "the arch transcendentalist."[29] But Christy simply excluded Whitman. He referred to Whitman only twice through the length of his study, and, even then, in contexts outside the discussion of American transcendentalism.[30] This oversight is pardonable since Christy admitted that his study was only "the first chapter" of a general investigation into "how far the American spirit had been impregnated, directly or indirectly, by the infiltration of Hindu thought during the XIXth century."[31]

Christy used the term Vedanta but did not define it. He was apparently unaware of Vedanta as a *system* of philosophy. What he called Vedanta in one context, he called "Hindu thought" in another.[32] Christy did not realize that "Hindu thought" is a very ambiguous term denoting six systems of philosophy and much else that emerged in a subcontinent called Hind. In confusing Vedanta with a general term like "Hindu thought," he was led to believe that the optimism of the transcendentalists has no parallel in Vedic literature and Vedantic philosophy. He spelled out this part of his thesis as follows:

Emerson and his friends read the Hindus for their idealistic philosophy, a philosophy naturally congenial to the Transcendental mind. But they were also practical Yankees facing the demands of a work-a-day world; so they read Confucius, a sage as shrewd as any Yankee, and found in him effective precepts whereby to regulate their affairs with men.[33]

The implication here is that Indian idealistic philosophy is short on the practical side of life. If we take Vedanta into consideration, this implied view of Christy will appear as still another of the misconceptions about India like Carpenter's view of "Asia."

28 *Ibid.,* p. ix.   29 (New York, 1957), p. xi.   30 Christy, pp. 132 and 270.

31 *Ibid.,* p. vii. It is interesting to note that it was from Romain Rolland that Christy received this challenge and not from Frederic I. Carpenter.

32 *Ibid.,* pp. 54, 56, and 88.   33 *Ibid.,* p. xi.

Sometimes, in comparing philosophical and theological systems, a scholar slips into a confusion of terminology. At times this happened to Christy. "Now, the human mind," he wrote, "has never produced an idealism as extreme as that of Vedanta, which would insist that the Absolute God is as much in Piccadilly Circus as in the most immaculate madonna."[34] His fault lay in confusing theistic concepts and terminology, such as "God," with Vedantic concepts, like "the Absolute." For, according to nondualistic Vedanta, the Absolute is merely the Absolute. The Absolute is not God. The Vedantic Absolute is undefinable, whereas God in every religious system is definable. Confessional creeds are a good example of man's attempts at defining God. The Vedantic Absolute is without attributes. God in every religious system, however, is known by his attributes. Misinterpretations of Vedanta have often arisen because of indiscriminate representation of Vedantic concepts. In the present study this confusion will be avoided.

Discussing Thoreau's asceticism, Christy mixed Chinese and "Hindu thought" and their influence on Thoreau. Tracing the reasons for Thoreau's retreat to Walden, he rightly remarked that we should understand Thoreau's religious philosophy as that of a Yogi. And then, he went on to expound this religious philosophy in the following words: "If it is true that Reality is Brahma—or the Over-Soul—and *the phenomenal world is a lie* [italics mine], then the logical end of life for one who believes in this is to seek devotedly that Reality."[35] The reasons for Thoreau's retreat according to Christy may or may not be true. But according to Vedanta the phenomenal world definitely is not a lie. It is *māya,* false, but only in relation to the Ultimate Reality. Christy, of course, was not conducting a study of Thoreau on the basis of Vedanta in its technical sense. He was simply reporting Thoreau's readings in the literatures of the alluring "Orient." At times, Christy, perhaps, for the above reason, missed the distinction between philosophy and mythology. An obvious example of this confusion appears in Christy's interpretation of Thoreau's translation of *Harivansa* from French into English. Here, Christy suggested that the legend of *The Transmigration of the Seven Brahmans* was a factor in converting Thoreau to the rigorous life of a Yogi.[36] Actually, this story treats superficially the doctrine of

[34] *Ibid.,* p. 74.
[35] *Ibid.,* p. 199.   [36] *Ibid.,* pp. 217-219.

transmigration of souls and concludes with a moral, forbidding the killing of a cow. That is to say, the story illustrates the trans-generational consequences of an evil deed. Moreover, this story as it is found in *Harivansa* is not part of Vedic literature. It is part of a folk tradition. Therefore, it need not be taken seriously. But Christy made use of it because through it he could interpret "Hindu thought" as requiring men to shun the pleasures of the world and attain a mystic union with the Ultimate Reality. What he failed to distinguish is the place of this legend in the body of post-Upaniṣadic tradition of a growing mythology as against the basic concepts of Vedantic philosophy.

Finally, in his concluding chapter, Christy lamented the un-popularity of Thoreau in the United States. He embarrasses the reader at this point by attributing Thoreau's unpopularity to the materialistic nature of American character. The embarrassment comes from his suggestion that temperamentally the Orient is mystical and the Occident practical. Thoreau, he argued, is mystical and, therefore, is popular in the Orient while he is ignored in his own country.[37] We have already noted how much labelling of the Orient as possessing a monopoly in mysticism is unjustified. It is unfair not only to the Orient but to the Occident as well. It is even unreal because, as far as mysticism is concerned, the world is not divided into Orient and Occident. These are arbitrary terms and have no specific meaning. Often they have been used in a romantic or derogatory sense. Therefore, in a consideration of American transcendental ideas, it becomes obligatory on the part of literary scholars to discard these vague terms and focus their interest on the specific system of Vedantic philosophy.

Prominent literary personages of his own times have perceived in Whitman's thought an affinity with Vedanta. Emerson is known to have remarked to F. B. Sanborn that *Leaves of Grass* was "a mixture of the *Bhagavad-Gita* and the New York *Herald*."[38] William N. Guthrie observed that Whitman's "Vedantic views are sometimes expressed with such originality and energy as to have brought a smile of delight to the serene immobile countenance of a Hindu friend. . . ."[39]

[37] *Ibid.,* pp. 232-233.

[38] William S. Kennedy, *Reminiscences of Walt Whitman* (London, 1896), p. 173.

[39] *Walt Whitman: the Camden Sage* (London, 1897), p. 25.

In 1856, shortly after the publication of *Leaves of Grass,* Thoreau met Whitman and greeted him with the compliment that his book was "wonderfully like the Orientals."[40] But Whitman professed a complete ignorance of "the Orientals" and asked Thoreau to tell him about them. Malcolm Cowley takes this denial literally and comments, "It is more than doubtful that he had even read the *Bhagavad-Gita,* one of the few books then available in translation."[41] Unlike Cowley, Gay Wilson Allen believes that Whitman's denial of any knowledge of the "Orientals" may have been disingenuous, or it could have been modesty before a man [Thoreau] who obviously knew a great deal about Oriental scriptures."[42] In refutation of Cowley's opinion we must recognize that Whitman's derivation of Vedantic views should not be limited to the *Bhagavad-Gita* alone. He could have come across those ideas in any of the available translations of the *Upaniṣads* and Vedic literature. Gay Wilson Allen points out in another place that "in 'A Backward Glance' (1888) Whitman claimed to have read 'the ancient Hindu poems' before writing the *Leaves of Grass.*"[43] We are not sure what these "ancient Hindu poems" are which were available to Whitman. He did not mention them in any of the numerous notes he kept.

That Whitman read Vedic literature is beyond doubt. There is overwhelming evidence that he did. The question is whether he read it before the publication of *Leaves of Grass* in 1855. The earliest translation of the *Bhagavad-Gita* was made in 1785 by Charles Wilkins. We have no proof that Whitman ever read this version. His own copy was a translation made by Cockburn Thomson and it did not come into his hands till 1857 when an English cork-cutter named Thomson Dixon gave it to him as a Christmas present. It is now in the Feinberg Collection and Whitman's marginal notes do not reveal any previous reading of it.[44]

If there is any special resemblance between Whitman's thought

---

[40] Malcolm Cowley, *Walt Whitman's "Leaves of Grass:" His Original Edition* (New York, 1959), p. xii.

[41] *Loc. cit.*

[42] *The Solitary Singer* (New York, 1955), p. 141.

[43] See his "Foreword" to V. K. Chari, *Whitman in the Light of Vedantic Mysticism* (Lincoln, Nebraska, 1964), p. vii.

[44] George Hendricks, "Whitman's Copy of the *Bhagavad-Gita,*" *Walt Whitman Review,* V (March 1959), pp. 12-14.

and art and the thought and art of any part of Vedic literature, it is between his *Leaves of Grass* and the *Bhagavad-Gita*. Whitman's denial of any knowledge of *Bhagavad-Gita* has baffled many of his critics who wanted to establish this resemblance. Dorothy F. Mercer maintains that though he did not read the *Bhagavad-Gita,* he was certainly familiar with Vedic literature, which, in her words is Sanskrit literature. "Whitman's own prose," she writes, "reveals an immediate knowledge of Sanskrit literature acquired before the publication of *Leaves of Grass* . . . the knowledge of Sanskrit acquired by Whitman, although unquestionable, is indefinable, and therefore, definite sources cannot be discussed."[45] Her deduction is that it is impossible to establish the precise sources of literary derivation of Whitman's Vedantic ideas. Therefore, she suggests that the "literary atmosphere" of Whitman's day was charged with Vedantic transcendental philosophy, and that he unconsciously absorbed it. In her words, "It was in this atmosphere, impregnated with interest in Hindu philosophy, literature, and religion that Whitman reached manhood."[46] Here she seems to imply that Whitman's contact with Vedic literature was indirect and unconscious. A similar view is also expressed by Malcolm Cowley who said: "It is true that they [Vedantic ideas] were vaguely in the air of the time and that Whitman may have breathed them from the Transcendentalists or even from some of the English quarterly reviews."[47] If opinions of this kind can be woven into a theory, it is one of "literary osmosis." Such a theory would also depict Whitman as a liar for telling Thoreau that he did not know the "Orientals." In fact, Walter K. Malone, who like Mercer and Cowley was unable to trace the exact sources of Whitman's Vedantic ideas, remarks that ". . . one cannot help but sense that Whitman was not being quite truthful"[48] about his ignorance of the *Bhagavad-Gita* prior to the publication of *Leaves of Grass* in 1855. What the osmosis theory points to is the express need to document the precise channels of Whitman's Vedantic derivation either from "the Transcendentalists" of New England or from

[45] Unpublished Ph.D. dissertation, *"Leaves of Grass* and the *Bhagavad-Gita*: A Comparative Study, " Univ. of California (1933), p. 1.

[46] *Ibid.,* p. 18.

[47] Whitman's *Leaves of Grass* (New York, 1959), p. xii.

[48] Unpublished Ph.D. dissertation, "Parallels to Hindu and Taoist Thought in Walt Whitman," Temple University (1964), p. 78.

"the English quarterly reviews" as Malcolm Cowley suggests.

One can easily argue that Emerson, Thoreau, and Whitman are dissimilar personalities reflecting their respective individualities in each of their writings. How could they possibly have a uniform kind of affinity with Vedantic philosophy? Emerson was staid and serene. He entered into disputes only with intellectuals on intellectual questions. His exit from the ministry was on intellectual grounds and the manner in which he removed himself from the Unitarian Church was quiet and deliberate. But when Thoreau disagreed, he was vehement. People reacted to him more violently than to Emerson. Unlike Emerson, Thoreau was austere and remained an ascetic throughout his life. He disdained blind conformity. In fact, Whitman thought that Thoreau wore a constant expression of disdain.[49] Whitman, on the other hand, was full of love for his fellowmen. He was anything but an ascetic. And unlike Emerson, he was not afraid of the profane. Therefore, one might ask, how the views of three different personalities could ever be consistent with a single system of philosophy like Vedanta. The answer lies in a proper understanding of the Vedantic worldview.

We have already discussed the inaccuracy of viewing East and West as monoliths so far as their thought and literature are concerned. We should keep in mind various systems of philosophy and various cycles in the history of literary activity in every civilization. With a view to promoting objectivity we must also acknowledge whatever distinctions exist in the philosophies and literatures of India. In philosophy, one finds six different systems, i.e., *Nyāya, Vaiśeṣika, Sānkhya, Yoga, Pūrvamīmāmsa,* and *Uttaramīmāmsa* or *Vedānta.*[50] Without keeping in mind the individual distinctions of these six systems, an evaluation of "Indian thought" would mislead any scholar. Dr. Albert Schweitzer, for instance, in his *Indian Thought and its Development,*[51] concluded that in Indian thought, "World and life negation

---

[49] Horace Traubel, *With Walt Whitman in Camden* (Boston, 1906), Vol. I, p. 212.

[50] M. Hiriyanna, *The Essentials of Indian Philosophy* (London, 1956), p. 46.

[51] Translated by Charles B. Russell (London, 1960); hereafter cited as Schweitzer.

occupy a predominant position".[52] It is possible that if one takes
the whole stretch of Indian thought, world and life negation
outweigh world and life affirmation. But in relation to the literature
and philosophy of the Vedic age even Schweitzer had to concede
that Indian worldview was not negative but positive. "In the
Upaniṣads", he wrote, "there is also a certain element of world
and life affirmation and in many writings in Indian literature
it even finds quite a strong expression".[53]

For the purpose of our present study, we should not lose sight
of Schweitzer's special remark concerning upaniṣadic philosophy,
because Vedanta essentially is the philosophy of the *Upaniṣads*.
Vedanta literally means *"Veda-end"* and denotes the place of
Upaniṣads in the collection of Vedic literature. In a metaphorical
sense, the *Upaniṣads* also contain the end or summation of the
message of the Vedas which is Vedantic philosophy.[54] In other
words, Vedanta is "the conclusion as well as the goal of the
Vedas".[55]

The *Upaniṣads* were written by different people during different
periods. They contain "heterogeneous matters".[56·] This is to say
that in them can be found germinal ideas for all the six systems
of philosophy which later developed in India. Suggestive of
this view are the words of a famous Indian scholar and philosopher
Dr. S. Radhakrishnan: "The Upaniṣads are respected not because
they are a part of *śruti* or revealed scripture and so hold a reserved
position, but because they have inspired generations of Indians
with vision and strength by their inexhaustible significance and
spiritual power".[57] One wonders if the *Upaniṣads* themselves
have any innate "spiritual power". Dialogues about Spirit, its
nature and its being, do occupy a predominant place in the
Upaniṣads. These dialogues may inspire many Indian readers
even today. But that is not the same thing as saying that "The
Upaniṣads . . . have inspired . . . Indians . . . by their inexhaustible strength and spiritual power".

[52] *Ibid.*, p. 3.   [53] *Loc. cit.*

[54] Winternitz, p. 204.

[55] S. Radhakrishnan, transl. and ed. *The Principal Upaniṣads* (London,
1953), p. 24. Also see S. Rangachar, *Outlines of the History of Classical
Sanskrit Literature* (Mysore, India, 1964), p. 15, for a literal meaning
of Vedanta.

[56] Winternitz, p. 213.

[57] *The Principal Upaniṣads* (London, 1953), p. 18.

The *Upaniṣads* are considered to be part of a body of Vedic literature known as *śruti*, literally, "heard". They are "heard" literature because they were recited by a *guru* to his disciple in an age when writing was not known in India and learning was transmitted orally. But over the generations the term *śruti* began to connote "revealed scripture". The *Vedas, Brahmaṇas, Āraṇyakas,* and *Upaniṣads* are now generally known as *śruti* or revealed scripture. These four collections of India's literature are available to us in the most primitive form of Sanskrit which is called Vedic Sanskrit. The Sanskrit of later literature came to be known as classical Sanskrit. Winternitz calls Vedic Sanskrit "Ancient High Indian", perhaps by analogy with Old High German.[58] He also describes Vedic literature as consisting of three classes of literary works, *the Veda samhitas, the Brahmaṇas,* and the *Āraṇyakas* and *Upaniṣads.*[59] S. Rangachar describes the same works as Vedic literature because they are available to us in Vedic Sanskrit.[60] In this sense the *Bhagavad-Gita* and Manu's *Manavadharmaśāstra* or the *Institutes of Manu* as the American transcendentalists knew it, are not Vedic literature. But they do illustrate Vedantic ideas. So does *Vishnu Purana.* And so does Jayadeva's *Gita-Govinda.* These works are written in Classical Sanskrit. Nevertheless, they strongly illustrate the Vedantic ideas. Therefore, for the purpose of our present study, we shall regard all Sanskrit literature containing Vedantic ideas which was translated into English before 1840 as Vedic literature.

We have taken liberties in defining Vedic literature, but we cannot take such liberties with the definition of Vedanta, because Vedanta is a system of philosophy. Vedantic ideas have their beginning in Vedic literature and were further developed in the *Upaniṣads.* Then they were finally systematized in A.D. 800 by Śankara in several treatises. According to Hiriyanna, the term Vedanta occurs in the *Upaniṣads,* but "while it there means only 'the final portion of the Vedas', it has since come to signify the subtle consciousness of the Veda taken as a whole. Accordingly Vedanta, in its later form, stands for the teaching not merely of the *Upaniṣads,* together with the earlier portions of the Veda,

---

[58] *Op. cit.,* p. 35.
[59] *Ibid.,* p. 46.
[60] *Outlines of the History of Classical Sanskrit Literature* (Mysore, India, 1964), p. 15.

but also of other parts of the sacred literature such as *Bhagavad-Gita* and *Vishnu Purana* which are regarded as reiterating and amplifying the Upaniṣadic doctrine".[61]   Therefore, to the extent that these literary works also reiterate and amplify Vedantic doctrine, we shall accept them as documents of the Vedantic system of philosophy.   It is in this sense that we should attempt to document the system of Vedantic ideas as found in the writings of American transcendentalists, Emerson, Thoreau, and Whitman.

The Vedantic worldview, then, is a view of the world as it is systematized in Vedantic philosophy and amplified in Vedic literature.   At this point we must explore some of the Vedantic concepts in order to determine the precise meaning of some of its technical terms as well as to understand the philosophy which would enable us to appreciate its worldview.

The first and foremost of these concepts is *Brahman*. Etymologically it is derived from the root *brh* which means "to grow or expand".[62]   Max Muller, perhaps, has this etymology in his mind when he explains: "Brahman meant originally force, will, wish, and the propulsive power of creation".[63]   This meaning gradually expands itself in its significance.   Hiriyanna explains this extension by interpreting that the root *brh* also stands for " . . . the power which of itself bursts into utterance as prayer; and it is to this meaning that . . . we should trace the philosophic significance of the term, *viz.,* the power or primary principle which spontaneously manifests itself as the Universe".[64]   Another philosopher defines it in these words: "Brahman which is the Sanskrit word for the Absolute, is the principle of search as well as the object sought, the animating ideal and its fulfilment.   The striving of the soul for the infinite is said to be Brahman.   The impulse that impels us to raise the question of the true, the divine, is itself divine".[65]   This idea of *Brahman* as the very urge to seek the Ultimate Truth is crucial in appreciating the departure of American Transcendentalists from inherited religious traditions. In the jargon of a dialectician, the same concept is explained:

[61] *The Essentials of Indian Philosophy* (London, 1956), p. 151.

[62] *Ibid.,* p. 20.

[63] "The Veda and Zend Avesta" in *The Vedas* (Calcutta, 1956), p. 5.

[64] *Op. cit.,* p. 20.

[65] S. Radhakrishnan, *Eastern Religions and Western Thought* (New York, 1960), p. 22.

"*Brahman* . . . is the cause of the origination, subsistence, and dissolution of the world which is extended in names and forms, which consists of many agents and enjoyers".[66] Thus it is both the material cause, *upadānakāraṇa,* and the efficient cause, *nimittakāraṇa,* of the world. Brahman is also conceived of as One without a second, self-existent, Absolute, eternal, and therefore, an object of meditation and not of religious worship.[67] "The word used in the *Upaniṣads* to indicate the Supreme (Ultimate and Irreducible) Reality is *Brahman*".[68] "Brahman is not merely a featureless Absolute. It is all this world".[69] *Brahman* then is not only the cause both of matter and spirit, but actual matter and spirit as well. But matter, of course, is not *Brahman* as our senses perceive. Our senses give it shapes, or rather, our senses perceive their material shapes, which is their appearance. *Brahman,* which is the ultimate cause of matter, is not removed from it but pervades it. Thus *Brahman* is said to have the nature of the Absolute, the final Being and, at the same time, the nature of the Creator, the Becoming. Because of this seemingly paradoxical nature of *Brahman,* Vedantists refer to *Brahman* as "That", and "It", and never as "He". This is understandable when we realize that in Sanskrit *Brahman* is a neuter singular noun.

The next Vedantic concept is *Ātman.* In the language of common sense, it is the essential being of man. It is both spiritual and physical. To suggest these qualities, it is often referred to as the "Self", or "Consciousness". As the essential being of man, it is not to be mistaken with the personal "I" or even the "I" which figuratively represents human community.

But even after grasping the definitions, we have to understand the relationships of *Brahman* to *Ātman* as expounded in the *Upaniṣads.* This is well summarized in the words of Paul Duessen who writes:

> . . . the fundamental thought of the entire Upanisad philosophy may be expressed by the simple equation:
>
> Brahman=Atman.

This is to say — the Brahman, the power which presents itself

66 S. Radhakrishnan, ed. *Brahma Sutra* (New York, 1960), p. 30.
67 Monier-Williams, *Sanskrit-English Dictionary.*
68 S. Radhakrishnan, *Principal Upaniṣads* (London, 1953), p. 52.
69 *Ibid.,* p. 64.

to us materialized in all existing things, which creates, sustains, preserves, and receives back into itself again all worlds, this eternal, infinite, divine power is identical with Atman, with that which, after stripping off everything external, we discover in ourselves as our real most essential being, or individual self, the soul. This identity of the Brahman and Atman, of God and the Soul, is the fundamental thought of the entire doctrine of the Upanisads. It is briefly expressed by the 'great saying' *tatvam asi,* 'That art Thou' (Chand. 6. 8. 7f); and *aham brahmāsmi,* 'I am Brahman' (Brih. i. 4. 10).[70]

This, then, is the basis of identity in the philosophy of the *Upaniṣads,* which, as we have noted earlier, is Vedanta. It is against this Vedantic concept of identity that we must measure the philosophy of identity in the writings of American transcendentalists.

But this identity of Brahman and Atman leaves the material and phenomenal world unexplained. The much needed explanation is supplied by the concept of *Māya. Māya* is naïvely and inadequately translated into English as "illusion". This naïveté led many early scholars to a belief that Vedanta taught that the material and phenomenal world is unreal, and therefore, it emphasized world negation and produced cynicism.

But modern scholars of Vedanta point out that the doctrine of *Māya* does not deny the world as unreal. In the words of one scholar, "The multiplicity of the universe, the unending stream of life is real, but only as a phenomenon".[71] What is denied by *Māya* is not the reality of the world, but only the ultimacy of this phenomenal world. The concept of *Māya* seems to serve a purpose which is explained by Heinrich Zimmer in these words: "The secret of Maya is this identity of opposites. Maya is a simultaneous-and-successive-manifestation of energies that are at variance with each other, processes contradicting and annihilating each other. . . ."[72] Therefore, *Māya* is not to be understood as a world and life negating doctrine, but as a principle which

[70] *The Philosophy of the Upaniṣads,* translated by Alfred S. Geden (Edinburg, 1906), p. 39.

[71] *Op. cit.,* p. 26.

[72] *Myths and Symbols in Indian Art and Civilization,* ed. by Joseph Campbell (New York, 1962), p. 46.

explains the identity of opposites.

In connection with the last point, we should note that where an attempt at finding identity in opposites is made, paradox emerges as a figure of speech. When we discuss the art and expression of the American transcendentalists we shall have an opportunity to study in depth the figure of paradox in literary expression.

This identity of *Brahman* and *Ātman,* spirit and matter, gives rise to ideas of simultaneous immanence and transcendence of Divinity in the universe. This is the special feature of Vedanta. Where these ideas prevail, there grows a special love for the world. Therefore, some scholars think that the philosophy of the *Upaniṣads* is not spiritualistic but materialistic.[73]

The peculiar identity of *Brahman* and *Ātman,* matter and spirit, is the basis of Vedantic monism. *Brahman* in this sense is describ-ed as "That One", *tat ēkam.* The individual, then, is part and parcel of "That All-One" without being different from "That One". When he loves another person or an object it is because the other person and the other object also are part and parcel of "That All-One". It is on this ground of identity that "I" and "Thou" relationships are established. "Everything is love for the sake of the Self".[74] Albert Schweitzer also acknowledges this as the basis of Vedantic ethics. "On the ground of identity", he writes, "of the I and Thou, as it follows from the doctrine of the Brahman, the Upaniṣads explain all love as self-love".[75] Identity of all men on the basis of their identity with and in Brahman is an important concept in explicating the attitudes of the American transcendentalists to their fellowmen.

Closely related to this doctrine of identity is the Vedantic explanation of evil. According to this school, evil is not absolute. It belongs to the world of relative values and is real only so far as those values are real. It belongs to the world of *Māya* only. Any one who has apprehended the Brahman, knows that unlike Brahman evil is not absolute. He becomes an exalted being. Before such a man Nietzsche's Superman is really insignificant.[76]

[73] P. T. Raju, *Indian Idealism and Modern Challenges* (Chandigarh, India, 1961), p. 8.

[74] V. B. Srikande, "The Nature of Self", *Recent Indian Philosophy,* edited by Kalidas Bhattacharya (Calcutta, 1963), p. 276.

[75] Schweitzer, p. 130. [76] *Ibid.,* p. 36.

The Superman of Nietzsche is superior only to ordinary men. But the one who has had a glimpse of Brahman is exalted above the contradictions of opposites, and is, therefore, either above or beyond Good and Evil. He is neither moved by good nor evil. He stands indifferent. In this sense also Vedantic world-view may be said to be optimistic and positive. The ideas of evil and original sin have no place in Vedanta. Emerson, Thoreau, and Whitman in different ways felt exalted. All three of them resented the doctrine of original sin. In the present study we shall try to measure the degree of sympathy that the Vedantic worldview received from them.

Ātman, when it loses sight of its identity with Brahman, is said to be caught up in the world of *Māya.* Such *Ātman* is suffering from ignorance, *Avidya.* As long as it continues in its bondage to ignorance, it is bound to follow a succession of births and rebirths in the form of various creatures. Out of this thinking arose the Vedantic doctrine of transmigration of souls. *Karma* was elaborated to justify this doctrine. Now, most scholars have translated and interpreted *Karma* naively as Fate. Indeed, Fate and Fatalism are related to the doctrine of *Karma.* But Fate is only the negative side of *Karma.* The positive side of this doctrine would insist that if one experiences the identity of *Ātman* and *Brahman,* for him there is no *Karma.* Indeed, *Karma* has been misinterpreted in India itself for too many centuries. It was used in justifying caste inequalities and also inequalities of wealth and opportunity. The poor, the sick, and the low-born were said to be reaping the consequences of *Karma* from their previous forms of existence. But this interpretation is post Upaniṣadic and is closely allied to the rise of mythology in the history of Indian thought. Since our concern in this study is Vedanta, we shall disregard the implications of mythology in the doctrine of *Karma.* In this sense Vedantic doctrine of *Karma* is merely the doctrine of "Compensation" for one's own actions for which he is answerable in more than one life.

In a consideration, then, of the Vedantic worldview, one must note the belief in the possibility of penetrating the world of inexplicable paradoxes in apprehending the ultimate identity of *Ātman* and *Brahman,* matter and spirit, good and evil, and of man and man. Such a belief cannot rest on rational conclusions. Hence, the mysticism of Vedanta. In Vedic literature, as we have defined it earlier, it is more a poetical mysticism than the doctrinaire mysticism of the later Yoga schools.

Having defined Vedic literature and having defined some of the terms that are used in Vedanta, we must now turn to a study of how they were made available to American men of letters. Without such a study mere interpretations of American transcendentalists in the light of Vedanta would be shallow. We must also note the monistic heritage in the Judeo-Christian religious background of American intellectual life. This monistic heritage is crucial in making Vedantic ideas acceptable to most Americans.

2

SOME VEDANTIC TENDENCIES IN THE RELIGIOUS HERITAGE OF AMERICA

IN THE American tradition there is an element of mysticism bearing a remote affinity with certain Vedantic concepts.[1] Some of the Puritan divines were mystics in spite of being realists. It is, therefore, worth enquiring whether this streak of mysticism had prepared American readers to receive cordially Vedic literature and Vedantic philosophy. The nature of American religious faith not unsurprisingly contains certain occasional monistic tendencies comparable to those of the theistic Vedantic *Bhakti* tradition. Despite the creedal and dogmatic structure of New England Puritanism, the elemental mysticism that knows no clime or age is in the very scriptures the Puritans meditated upon daily. It is a mysticism not simply of the dramatic conversion of sinners to saints. It is a mysticism that is reminiscent of rare monistic tendencies of Christianity and its parent Judaism. It finds its best expression in the words of Jesus, "I and the Father are one".[2] This claim epitomizes the essence of nondualistic Vedanta. If the "I" of Jesus is interpreted as *Ātman,* and the "Father" as *Brahman,* this assertion may be described as the Upaniṣadic truth, *aham brahmāsmi,* I am *Brahman.*

One may say that even in the Old Testament tradition this idea was conceived of as Immanuel, God with us.[3] The Kabbalah tradition points out that the Hebraic concept of *shekinah* describes God as residing or being immanent in the universe while he is also transcendent.[4]

---

[1] William James, *The Varieties of Religious Experience* (New York, 1945), p. 419.

[2] St. John, 10:30.

[3] Isaiah, 7:11, 9:8.

[4] George Vijda, "The Dialectic of Talmud and the Kabbalah", *Diogenes* (Fall, 1967), p. 64.

Against this background Christianity inherited the concept of God's simultaneous transcendence and immanence. When Jesus said "I and the Father are one", he compressed the philosophy of identity as well. Without such a philosophy, there can be no stable foundation for his good news of love and universal brotherhood. In his gospel, love stands for identity. The American transcendentalists inherited this doctrine of identity and love. Their Puritan and Quaker fathers recognized this identity between God and man. This strengthened, often, the belief in their special calling. And despite the Calvinist belief in God's elect, the Puritan divines gave mystic expression to the nearness of God's presence and some even felt that God has an identity with his creation.

But in the doctrine of Original Sin and the consequent doctrine of Grace, there was a formidable obstacle to the Puritan hope of mystic union with God. Original Sin, the Puritans believed, created a chasm between them and their God. Therefore, they could only worship God as the object of their meditation. But in unguarded moments some of them lost this distinction between subject and object and experienced a kind of mystic union with God which is a discovery of identity. Thus we find Jonathan Edwards recording in his "Personal Narrative" a longing for being "rapt up to him in heaven, and be as it were swallowed up in him for ever!" Later, he experienced a kind of vision in which he was "sweetly rapt and swallowed up in God", as he conversed with Christ. Even Conrad Cherry, who denies that Jonathan Edwards was a mystic, admits that he sometimes employed a Neoplatonic metaphysic to suggest " a monism in which the distinction between uncreated being and created being is not always clear".[5]

Moreover, what is attractive in Edwards is that, except when he was absorbed in controversy, "his reconstruction of Calvinism often took the form of an attempt at synthesis of the main lines of thought in traditional theism and classical pantheism. He was searching his mind always for an adequate 'third way' that would overcome the much-too-easy alternative between the two views".[6]

[5] *The Theology of Jonathan Edwards*: *A Reappraisal* (Garden City, N. Y., 1966), p. 86.

[6] Douglas Elwood, *The Philosophical Theology of Jonathan Edwards* (New York, 1960), p. 7.

This habit of looking for the "third way" is the earliest manifestation of American eclecticism. Edwards tried to reconcile Locke and Plato, Calvinism and spiritual mysticism. From this, one may infer that his thought took root and developed into New England transcendentalism.

According to Perry Miller, Edwards in his *Dissertation Concerning the End for which God Created the World* pointed to a doctrine that verges on pantheism. Miller summarizes its thesis as follows:

> ... God did not create the world, said Edwards, merely to exhibit his glory; He did not create it out of nothing simply to show that He could: He who is Himself the source of all being, the substance of life, created the world out of Himself by diffusion of Himself into time and space. He made the world, not by sitting outside and above it, by modelling it as a child models sand, but by an extension of Himself, by taking upon Himself the forms of stones and trees and of man.[7]

Miller's use of phrases like "diffusion of Himself" and "extension of Himself" are highly suggestive of the Vedantic doctrine of creation by Emanation. A view of the world based on such a belief in Emanation, often, allows for a belief in Immanence of God in the objective world and, therefore, a belief in the possibilities of mystical religious experience in which, in the words of Conrad Cherry, "the distinction between uncreated being and created being is not always clear". Such a belief approximates to the Vedantic identity between created and uncreated being. But it is well known that Edwards was an ardent defender of Calvinism. One may speculate that Miller's interpretation of Edwards' *Dissertation Concerning the End for which God Created the World* was an instance of a devout Calvinist leaning towards the innate monism of the Gospel of Jesus.

An earlier instance of the Puritan who clung to traditional Church dogma but on occasions longed for and cherished his mystic experience is Edward Taylor. His third sermon in *Christographia* explains in a rational way the oneness of God and Christ.[8] Towards the end of the sermon he exhorts his listeners: "O then Strive to be one with him. United to him in a Saving

---

[7] *NEQ*, XIII (December 1940), p. 603.

[8] Ed. Norman S. Grabo (New Haven, 1962), pp. 75-105.

Union; If thou attainest to this, then the End of the personall Union, will be attained by thee".[9]   In urging his listeners to a "personall Union", Taylor comes close to the followers of the Bhakti school of Vedanta.[10]   Taylor's words may be interpreted as follows: God the Father is divine and so is God the Son.   If you believe in the Son and attain a personal union with Him, you shall also attain a personal union with the Father. In striving "to be one with Him", one could realize his oneness with Ultimate Reality.   Devotion to the personal God Jesus makes this oneness possible.   Taylor's exhortation is similar to Lord Krishna's in the 55th verse of the 18th Chapter of *Bhagavad-Gita*: "Through devotion [to a personal god, Iśvara] he [a devotee] comes to know Me, what my measure is and who I am in truth; then, having known Me in truth, he forthwith enters into Me".[11] This is the essence of Vedantic Bhakti tradition.   One may attain mystic union with Ultimate Reality through devotion to a personal god. To the Puritan divines, Jesus was the personal God and they seem to have believed, like Taylor, that through devotion to Jesus, mystic union with God the father was possible.

In India, the tradition of *Bhakti* inspired a literature of meditations, songs of praise, and allegories.   In the Bhakti allegories, of course, the devotee always is a maiden craving union with her beloved.   Naturally such songs employed sensuous imagery and their style, like Taylor's is baroque.   Such *Bhakti* allegories like Jayadeva's *Gita Govinda* were not known to Taylor.   What was known to him was the *Song of Solomon,* which he called the *Canticles.*   He used its imagery and allegorized the longings of his soul for God as the longings of the bride for the bridegroom. Of necessity, the theme of such poems is love.   The first stanzas of his First "Meditation" epitomizes this theme which he extends through most of his writings.

What Love is this of thine, that Cannot bee
  In thine Infinity, O Lord, Confide,
Unless it in thy very person bee,
  Infinity and Finity Conjoyn'd?
What hath thy Godhead, as not satisfied

[9] *Ibid.,* p. 104.   [10] See *Vedanta Dictionary.*
[11] Ed. S. Radhakrishnan (London, 1960), p. 371.

Marri'de our Manhood, making it its Bride?[12]

Love is the symbolic ingredient in the paradoxical union of "Infinity" and "Finity" and of "Godhead" and "manhood." This ingredient, in Christian terminology, is sometimes described as the Grace of God and typified by the love of the Bridegroom for the Bride. In the literature of Vedantic Bhakti school it is simply "love," sometimes with strong erotic connotations, and is typified by Lord Krishna's love for his beloved Radha.

Such longings of love can spring only from a belief in the immanence or in the indwelling spirit of God, because only such a belief could persuade a man to hope for a mystic experience in which the identities of subject and object are blurred. In the second stanza of an undated poem "Experience," Edward Taylor evokes the ineffability of a mystic experience:

> Most strange it was! But yet more strange that shine
>   Which filled my Soul then to the brim to spy
> My Nature with thy Nature all Divine
>   Together joyn'd in Him that's Thou, and I.
> Flesh of my Flesh, Bone of my Bone, There's run
> Thy Godhead, and my Manhood in thy son.[13]

Using Christian metaphors of trinity and marriage, Taylor conveys the idea of a mystic experience. He seems to imply a sense of exaltation as well. "My Nature with thy Nature all Divine" is what any Vedantic mystic would say in the most explicit terms. In Taylor's "Experience" the distinctions of subject and object are almost lost. Taylor, as a Puritan theologian, would not, of course, say "I am God" as did Emerson much later. His mind is attuned to the trinitarian patterns of thought and he would justify his mystic experience only through the Grace of "thy Son." At the same time he feels exalted and elevated above the angels. He sounds like a superman in the fourth stanza of "Experience:"

> I'le Claim my Right; Give place, ye Angells Bright,
>   Ye further from the Godhead stand than I.

[12] *The Poems of Edward Taylor,* ed. by Donald E. Stanford (New Haven, 1960), p. 1.
[13] *Ibid.,* pp. 8, 9.

My Nature is your Lord; and doth Unite
  Better than yours into thy Deity.
God's throne is first and mine is next; to you
  Onely the place of Waiting-men is due.[14]

Indeed the assertion "My Nature is your Lord" comes close to
the Vedantic conclusion *"aham brahmasmi,"* I am *Brahman.* One
might say that at this point, Edward Taylor is expressing the Vedantic principle of identity of Atman and Brahman in Biblical
terminology and in Christian imagery. But the Calvinistic climate
of his day did not allow him to sustain this newly attained sense
of exaltation for long. His theology reminded him constantly of
his fall through Original Sin and he humbled himself before God
and said, "I do condemn myself before thy Grace."[15] The Vedantin who glances at the glory of *Brahman* in mystic experience feels
so exalted that he regards himself a Superman. For the sake of
convenience we shall call him a *Brahmanical* Superman. As we
have noticed in the first chapter, such a man places himself above
all men and even above mythological Gods. He could develop a
sense of aloofness from his fellowmen as did Thoreau. Edward
Taylor certainly did not stay aloof from his fellowmen. But he
exalted himself above the angels. One finds in him a perceptible
kinship of attitude with the *Brahmanical* Superman.

    In his writings Taylor occasionally employed the figure of para-
dox much in the manner in which the Upaniṣads employ it as a
poetic device. Taylor and the poets of the *Upaniṣads* seem to be
trying their level best to describe the ineffability of experiencing
the Ultimate Reality which Taylor calls Lord, and the Upaniṣadic
poets *Brahman.* His "Meditation 2" is a good example:

My Deare, Deare, Lord I do thee Saviour Call:
  Thou in my Soul art, as I Deem,
Soe High, not High enough, Soe Great; too small;
So Deare, not Deare enough in my esteem.
So noble, yet So Base: too Low; Too Tall:
Thou Full, and Empty art: Nothing, yet All.[16]

The poem is saved from blasphemy only because of its intensely
devotional context. But the tone of nearness and attachment to

[14] *Ibid.,* p. 9.   [15] *Ibid.,* p. 413.   [16] *Ibid.,* pp. 5, 6.

God is unmistakably evoked. The sufficiency of God is balanced against the poet's need for more of the same. The Upaniṣads employ a similar device of paradox to indicate the omnipresence of God. "Atman, smaller than the small, greater than the great, is hidden in the hearts of all living creatures." "It is attained by him alone whom It chooses."[17] Paradox as a figure of speech comes naturally to mystics. It is a device which Emerson employs with great skill in "Brahma."[18]

Edwards and Taylor, however, did not derive their mysticism from the Vedantins. Rather their mysticism is rare and guarded, not explicit and deliberate like the mysticism of the Vedantins and the nineteenth century American transcendentalists. One may opine that their mystic religious experience is indicative of their rare acknowledgement of oneness with God. The idea of Ultimate oneness or identity, in so far as it is related to the belief in a God immanent, is an innate impulse buried deeply in Judeo-Christian heritage as Floyd Stovall pointed out in *American Idealism.*[19]

In Pennsylvania a different kind of religious experience took place during the Colonial times. Its central figure William Penn was a Quaker and his colony was peopled by believers who were already liberated from Calvinist dogmatism. George Fox the founder of Quakerism outgrew Calvinism and developed the doctrine of direct revelation. Perry Miller maintained that from the idea of regeneration, Quakers derived the doctrine of direct revelation and a belief in intuition.[20] He discovered early that there is no distinction between his own consciousness and that of God.[21] He believed that the Holy Spirit dwelt in every man. He called it the Inner Light. By contemplating it one may commune with God and intuit His will. The Inner Light that resides in man makes him dear to every other man. This is almost monistic in outlook

---

[17] *Katha Upaniṣad,* I, ii, 20, 23.

[18] "Emerson's Poetry: A Study of Form and Techniques," unpublished Ph.D. Dissertation by Richard A. Yoder, University of Pennsylvania, 1967, p. 204.

[19] (Norman, Oklahoma, 1943), p. 6.

[20] "Jonathan Edwards to Emerson," *NEQ,* XIII (December 1940), p. 599; also see William C. Braithwaite, *The Beginnings of Quakerism* (Cambridge, England, 1955). pp. 1-22.

[21] Raechel Knight, *The Founder of Quakerism: A Psychological Study of the Mysticism of George Fox* (London, 1922), p. 251.

and approximates to the Vedantic doctrine of ultimate identity of all creation despite differences in material appearance. This has been the basis of Vedantic doctrine of compassion. Once again, one finds a difference in terminology. The Inner Light of the Quakers may properly be called *Ātman* in Vedantic jargon. Just as the Quaker, by silent contemplation on the Inner Light communes with God, so does the Vedantin contemplate inwardly on the *Ātman* until he realizes its essential identity with *Brahman* in a mystic communion. It is because of the presence of *Ātman* in every creature that all forms of life become respectable and adorable. The Quaker view of compassion on fellow-creatures at times seems to approach the Vedantic.

As suggested before, the idea of God's presence in man is related to the idea of God's immanence or God's omnipresence. Such an idea generally leads to a belief in God's presence in Nature. This usually becomes the basis of such doctrines as "identity" and "correspondence." This process can be seen in the experience of some Quakers in America. The Puritans too believed that God was omnipresent and they looked upon nature as acting out the will of God. Nature and the universe testified to the wisdom and power of God. They little suspected that later this attitude would emerge as romanticism usurping the supremacy of Calvinistic theology.[22]

While the Puritans obliquely expressed their belief in the possibilities of a mystical union with their God, the Quakers explicitly taught the desirability of such an experience. In the language of George Fox and his followers, the mystical experience is Illumination. It corresponds to the Vedantin's experience of *Samādhi*. The result of this experience is a recognition of identity with the Creator and the Created. This recognition is shown in the compassion of the individual. Such was the attitude of John Woolman towards all men and all fellow creatures. Whittier found Woolman's compassion comparable to that of a Vedantin called Vishnu Śarman, the author of *Hitopadeśa*.

"What is religion?" asks the old Hindu writer of Vishnu Sharman [apparently Whittier mistook the author's name for the title of the book] "Tenderness toward all creatures." Or, as

[22] Perry Miller, *The New England Mind: the Seventeenth Century* (Cambridge, Mass., 1967), p. 241.

Woolman expressed it, "Where the love of God is verily perfected, a tenderness toward all creatures made subject to our will is experienced. . . ."[23]

Whittier's comment substantiates the theory that some beliefs and attitudes in American religious experience bear a valid resemblance to Vedantic principles. Unlike the Calvinists and more like the Vedantins, Woolman's Quakerism led him to say: " 'I found no narrowness respecting Sects and Opinions, but believe that sincere upright-hearted people, in every society that truly love God are accepted of Him.' "[24] Any Vedantin would maintain a similar acceptance of other sects and opinions. In matters of religious tolerance, the Quaker tradition in American religious experience helped swing the pendulum away from dogmatic faith. Despite this Quaker tolerance of other faiths, Woolman did not compromise with an evil system. He became something of a radical reformer in persuading his listeners to free their slaves. Mahatma Gandhi, a product of Vedantic tolerance, took a similar reformist stand against "Untouchability" in India.[25] Both of them manifest the force of the idea of God's identity with his creation. A philosophy based on such identity is bound to cause many side-effects, mostly social and reformist. It may be because of such effects that orthodox established religion resents such a philosophy and brands it a new form of infidelity.

Woolman did not expound his philosophy systematically. But from his own compassionate attitude towards man, bird, and beast, it may be deduced that his philosophy transcends dogma, prejudice, social and political custom, and identifies creation with the Creator. This is the monistic foundation of Woolman's gospel of love. It is based on a recognition of identities.

The founding Quakers were bold explorers. George Fox himself urged the study of "the nature of birds, roots, plants, and trees." This interest fanned out into a multitude of activities not the least of which was prospecting for new plants and raising them

[23] John G. Whittier, "Introduction" to his edition of *The Journal of John Woolman* (Boston, 1871), p. 10, fn.

[24] Edwin H. Cady, *John Woolman: the Mind of a Quaker Saint* (New York, 1966), p. 52.

[25] Reginald Reynolds, *The Wisdom of John Woolman* (London, 1948), p. 17.

in private botanical gardens.[26] Also in this line lay the travels and discoveries of John and William Bartram. John Bartram was not a literary man but he was a pioneer botanist and explorer whose *Observations* (1751) took him from Pennsylvania to Onandaga, Oswego, and Lake Ontario and subsequently to the South, the result of which he recorded in his *Descriptions of East Florida* (1769). William Bartram accompanied his father. But his own *Travels* written in the 1780's was not published till 1791. In this book his observations were limited not simply to scientific studies. He had inherited the Quaker worldview that is founded on compassion to fellow creatures and like most of his fellow believers expressed his faith in a God who is immanent in Nature. Or, he may have believed, like Jonathan Edwards, that Nature is an emanation of Being. This idea seems basic to his compassionate attitude towards all forms of life including fish, birds, bears, snakes, as well as Negroes and Indians. He prayed at times, to the "sovereign lord" who endowed "man with power and preeminence here on earth, and establish[ed] his dominion over all creatures" that "man's understanding be so illuminated with wisdom . . . that we may be enabled . . . to perform our duty towards those submitted to our service and protection, and be merciful to them even as we hope for mercy."[27] His pleas for a considerate treatment of Indians are often dismissed by critics as an eighteenth-century romantic fashion. But in actual fact they are more than that. He grew up in a home where the slaves were set free and were invited to sit at the family table for dinner daily. As a person faithful to his own beliefs, he retained his sense of solidarity with fellow human beings. The foundations of his human compassion are in the Quaker conviction that God is immanent in every creature.

In his descriptions of Nature, William Bartram conveys a mystic's sense of wonder in the august presence of an immanent Being. Here is an example:

What power of faculty is it, that directs the cirri of the Cucurbita, Momordica, Vitis and other climbers, towards the twigs

[26] Harold Loukes, *The Discovery of Quakerism* (London, 1960), pp. 163, 164.

[27] N. Bryllion Fagin, *William Bartram: Interpreter of the American Landscape* (Baltimore, 1933), pp. 51-52.

of shrubs, trees and other friendly support? We see them invariably leaning, extending and like the fingers of the human eyes to see with; and when their hold is fixed, to coil the tendril in a spiral form, by which artifice it becomes more elastic and effectual, than if it had remained in direct line, for every revolution of the coil adds a portion of the strength; and thus collected, they are enabled to dilate and contract as occasion or necessity requires, and then by yielding to, and by humoring the motion of the limbs and twigs, or other support on which they depend, are not so liable to be torn off by sudden blasts of wind or to her assaults; is it sense or instinct that influences their actions? it must be some impulse; or does the hand of the Almighty act and perform this work in our sight?[28]

This passage represents, more or less precisely his attitude towards Nature as well as his manner of writing. Attitude and style appear to be interdependent in a sincere man like William Bartram. He wonders what "faculty" it is that directs the cirri of various climbers. His answer is in the form of rhetorical question, "does the hand of the Almighty act and perform this work in our sight?" Such a rhetorical question could be raised by anyone who perceives the immanence of God in Nature. And then, there is that closeness of detail interspersed with speculation in a figurative language, "as if they had eyes to see with." These devices serve to amplify his observation. What is important to note here is that to a person like him who believes in an immanent God, details of Nature become most important, for, in every detail God's omnipresence is manifested. In this respect there is a particular similarity with the manner of the Vedantins. This does not mean that William Bartram subscribed to every doctrine of the Vedantins. It only means that to the extent he speculated about the presence of the "Almighty" in the growth behavior of the cirri and such delicate tendrils of plants, he held a view of Nature that approximates the Vedantic belief in Immanent Being.

In some respects Thoreau's "Natural History of Massachusetts"[29] may be compared to William Bartram's *Travels*. The

[28] *The Travels of William Bartram*, ed. by Mark Van Doren (New York, 1928), p. 19.

[29] Henry D. Thoreau, *Works* (Boston, 1906), vol. 5; hereafter cited as T. *Works*.

modern reader tends to concentrate on the central theme of Thoreau's joy in the world of Nature. In the last five paragraphs of this work, he chides the authors of Natural History for being prosaic.

A passage in *Maine Woods,* for instance, bears a special resemblance in attitude and style to that quotation from William Bartram:

> It is a country full of evergreen trees, of mossy silver birches and watery maples, the ground dotted with insipid small, red berries, and strewn with damp and moss-grown rocks,—a country diversified with innumerable lakes and rapid streams ... the forest resounding at rare intervals with the note of the chickadee, the blue jay, and the woodpecker, the scream of the fishhawk and the eagle, the laugh of the loon. . . . Who shall describe the inexpressible tenderness and immortal life of the grim forest, where Nature, though it be midwinter, is ever in her spring, where Moss-grown and decaying trees are not old, but seem to enjoy a perpetual youth; and blissful innocent Nature, like a serene infant, is too happy to make noise, except by a few tinkling rills?
>
> What a place to live, what a place to die and be buried in! There, certainly men would live for ever, and laugh at death and grave.[30]

In his *Journals,* too, he writes several passages expressing wonder at the identity he has with Nature. [31] Here is an example:

> Aug. 17 [1851]. For a day or two it has been quite a cool. . . . This coolness comes to condense the dews and clear the atmosphere. The stillness seems most deep and significant. Each sound seems to come from out a greater thoughtfulness in nature, as if nature had acquired some character and mind. The cricket, the gurgling stream, the rushing wind amid trees, all speak to me soberly yet encouragingly of the steady onward progress of the universe. My heart leaps into my mouth at the sound of the wind in the woods. I, whose life was but yesterday

[30] *Ibid.,* vol. 3, pp. 89-90.
[31] Walter Harding, *A Thoreau Handbook* (New York, 1959), pp. 44, 45 and 136.

so desultory and shallow, suddenly recover my spirits, my spirituality, through my hearing.[32]

Here, as in the passage from Bartram, one finds a catalogue of details, which seem to put Thoreau in a speculative mood, "Each sound seems to come from out a greater thoughtfulness in nature, as if nature had acquired some character and mind." And Thoreau begins to recover suddenly "my spirits, my spirituality, through my hearing." William Bartram wondered if "the hand of the Almighty" guided the growth of the cirri. Thoreau wondered "if nature had acquired some character and mind." In his speculations and in cataloguing details Thoreau appears to follow the tradition of William Bartram. Both of them appear to display an attitude and style that is similar to the attitude and style of the anonymous writers of Vedic literature as suggested earlier.

Unfortunately, Harold Hintz, who wrote *The Quaker Influence in American Literature*,[33] ignored William Bartram. If his thesis that Quaker influence molded the thought and character of Tom Paine and Emerson is valid, then it is no less true that Bartram's example anticipated the thought and character of Thoreau to a considerable extent.

One may conclude that the idea of God's immanence released the Puritans occasionally, and the Quakers more frequently, from their commitment to the doctrine of Original Sin and Fallen Creation. It made their successors more receptive to any literature and system of philosophy which embodied more directly a doctrine of the immanent God, direct revelation and religious individualism. But the early Americans had to wait. It was only after the concentrated efforts of Sir William Jones had brought forth some of the most delightful translations of Sanskrit literature, that Americans with a mystic bent of mind realized how much they had in common with the Vedantins. It is appropriate, therefore, to examine in the following chapter the reputation of Sir William Jones in America and see how that helped spread the word of discovery of Vedic literature and Vedantic philosophy.

---

[32] Henry D. Thoreau, *Journals,* ed. by Bradford Torrey and Francis H. Allen (Cambridge, Mass., 1949), vol. 2, pp. 390-391; hereafter T. *J.*
[33] (New York, 1940), p. 24.

3

EARLY AMERICAN INTEREST IN THE LIFE AND WORKS OF SIR WILLIAM JONES

IN THE preceding chapter we have seen the ascendance of monistic concepts in American thought and noted how the climate was conducive to the reception of the overt monism of Vedanta. Vedanta, however, did not reach America by way of the European Judeo-Christian religious heritage. It arrived through the work of comparative philologists. Often, a scholar traditionally takes interest in the literature and philosophy of another civilization purely for the scholarly purpose of comparing literary forms and philosophical ideas. Early American interest in Vedic literature and Vedantic philosophy appears to have developed for very different reasons.

First, British imperialism encounters Hindu civilization and begins to study and master it. At about the same time the American colonies which have inherited part of the British legal and administrative system break away from British rule. Humanists like Sir William Jones sympathize with the American struggle for independence and try to prevent war between Britain and the Colonies. Thus, for political reasons, a prominent British jurist who has already been known in America for his legal treatizes and political pamphlets favoring American independence, becomes even more popular in early America. Then, he goes to India, taking with him his zeal for preserving and guaranteeing general human dignity and liberty through law. Once in India, he imposes upon himself the tremendous task of interpreting Sanskrit literature and Hindu civilization to Britain with a view to preventing misinformed and unintended colonial tyranny. Because he was already known in America as a friend of its ideals of liberty and equality, his interpretive works become as popular in America as have been his earlier legal and political treatizes. His humanitarian political views and his scholarly translations of Vedic literature and interpretations of Vedantic philosophy bring him admiration. Therefore, it is relevant to consider briefly early American interest in Jones's life and works.

Far too often the role of literature in bringing about the integration of cultures and civilizations and in paving the way towards a sense of human solidarity is neglected by scholars. The importance of the life and works of Sir William Jones lay in that "it was given to him to perform a most conspicuous service to his fellowmen in making our diverse national inheritances in culture One Great and Common Heritage for all men in all climes."[1]

Born on September 28, 1747, of parents interested in mathematics, he lost his father when he was only three years old. Thereafter, his mother guided his learning with mathematical precision. Early when he showed curiosity in a particular subject, his mother would say, "Read, and you will know." Thus at the earliest age, he received the foundations of a scholar. He was precocious and soon overcame the handicap of an accidentally-blinded right eye by developing a remarkable memory. At the age of four he was able to quote Shakespeare. At Harrow, which he entered at the age of eight, he made impressive progress. Here he first established his reputation as a linguist. He was taught Latin and Greek at school but he taught himself French, Spanish, and Italian. When he wanted to read the Bible in the original, he taught himself Hebrew. This in turn led him to Middle-Eastern literatures and soon he was studying Arabic. At seventeen, when he joined University College, Oxford, he discovered the superb collection of Arabic literature at the Bodleian. With the help of a Syrian named Mirza, he soon attained facility in reading and writing Arabic.[2] At this stage he was only a step short of the fabulous riches of Persian literature. Soon he learned Persian, too, and discovered the sensuous poetry of Hafiz, Saadi, and Firdausi. He even thought of rejuvenating with romantic subjects English poetry which in the mid-eighteenth century, in the opinion of many scholars, was stagnating in the neoclassical tradition of con-

[1] Suniti K. Chatterji, "Sir William Jones: 1746-1794," in *Sir William Jones: Bicentenary of His Birth Commemoration Volume, 1746-1946* (Calcutta, 1948), p. 96.

[2] Garland Cannon, *Oriental Jones* (New York, 1964), p. 10; biographical information has been drawn from this book and *DNB*.

trolled emotion. Besides, he wanted to explore the humanistic qualities of the Middle-Eastern cultures.

In 1768 Christian VII of Denmark was looking for a competent translator for the manuscript copy in his possession of Mirza Shah's *Ta'rikh-i-Nadiri*. King Christian brought the manuscript to London. The British government then sent it to Jones with a request to turn it into French. Jones, however, was not excited. He never really admired absolute monarchs and he did not believe that Nadir Shah deserved a high place in history. So, at first, he let it be known, rather indiscreetly, that the manuscript was the last thing in the world that he would have translated. All the same, after much tedious labor, he finally translated it at his own expense in 1770. This work entitled *L'Histoire de Nader Chah,* brought him immediate recognition as a learned "Orientalist" and he was elected to the Royal Society of Copenhagen. To this translation, he added his famous "Traité sur la Poësie Orientale," and achieved his first objective of introducing the Middle East to Europe, thus paving way for an expanded idea of humanity and human culture.

But this early "Orientalism" did not assure him of a lucrative career. His mother had made great financial sacrifices and he was obligated to her. The only way he could rise to her expectations was to become a lawyer. So in 1770 he took up law studies at the Middle Temple. This study, he hoped would make him a distinguished lawyer and possibly a statesman. But even while he was studying law he published five works on "Oriental" themes: *The Grammar of the Persian Language* (1771), *Dissertation sur la littérature Orientale* (1771), *Lettre a Monsieur A*** du P**** (1771), *Poems* (1772), and *Poeseos Asiaticae Commentariorum* (1774). The 1771 edition of *The Grammar of the Persian Language* was acquired by the Yale University Library before 1810 and by the University of Michigan Library after 1810. James Warley Miles, a missionary to the Near East, also bought it early enough to enable Charleston College Library to acquire it from him in 1854. The second edition of 1775 was bought by James Vaughan of Philadelphia, Pa., and he donated it to the American Philosophical Society Library around 1800. There is no proof, however, that James Vaughan was deeply interested in Persian and other non-European languages and literatures. The third edition of 1783, the fourth of 1801, the fifth of 1809 were acquired by thirteen major libraries in the United States—all prior to 1820.[3] These acquisitions indicate the beginnings of American interest in the scholarly researches of Jones and testify to a slow but growing interest in non-European literatures. *Poems, Consisting Chiefly of Translations from the Asiatick Languages* (1772) by Jones, for instance, was acquired by nine major libraries in the United States prior to 1800. A later edition (1777) was acquired by five more libraries, again, before the turn of the century. This is further proof of early American interest in Jones's investigations into non-European literatures. Jones's *Poeseos Asiaticae Commentariorum* of 1774 was owned by Thomas Jefferson and is now in the Library of Congress in Washington, D.C. In Philadelphia alone three important libraries (the American Philosophical Society Library, the Library Company of Philadelphia, and the University of Pennsylvania Library) acquired copies of this early edition prior to 1828. These acquisitions are illustrative of the intensifying interest of American scholars in the unfamiliar literatures of Asia. One does not find in the five works of Jones mentioned above any direct reference to Vedic literature. But, in these works Jones achieved a calculated effect. He prepared European and the farther-flung American readers to shed their ignorance of non-European literatures and eagerly await genuine translations of original works of art. For instance, in the *Poems* of 1772, he included "The Palace of Fortune: An Indian Tale" based on Alexander Dow's *Tales Translated from the Persian of Inatulla.* Jones derived this Hindu poem from a tertiary source and at this stage he had no idea either of Sanskrit language or its literature. Nevertheless, through Persian, he was encouraged to explore further into the heritage of India.

In 1773 Jones was admitted to the London Literary Club at the same time as David Garrick. The Club was proud of his linguistic and literary accomplishments and his level-headed humanism attracted the affection of Dr. Samuel Johnson and Mrs. Thrale.[4]

As has been pointed out early in this chapter, Jones's disdain for absolutist monarchs led him to detest the policies of George III towards the American colonies. In the middle seventies this

[3] For a detailed account of US Library holdings of this work, see Appendix.

[4] Cannon, *Oriental Jones,* pp. 41-42.

brought him into the fold of Whig sympathizers for American independence. In addition to his fame in America as a seeker of American and British conciliation, Jones acquired a substantial American reputation as a lawyer. Till the late eighteenth century American legal system depended on the British common law and British legal commentaries. Jones's *An Essay on the Law of Bailments,* published in 1781, became a standard textbook on the subject. It became so popular, in fact, that in America alone it went through as many as seven pirated editions between 1796 and 1836. Thomas Jefferson owned a copy of this work published by Samuel Etheridge at Boston in 1796.[5] Certainly the elite leadership of the American Revolution did share several ideals with Jones besides the usual empathy of scholars. An American legal historian, David Hoffman, said of Jones: "Had he never written anything but his Essay on Bailments, he would have left a name unrivalled in the common law, for philosophical accuracy, elegant learning, and finished analysis."[6]

His popularity in America as a lawyer was heightened by his sympathies with the ideals of American democracy. He became known as a humanist with a sense of fair play. He soon found himself in the company of people with similar attitudes. The most famous of such men was Bishop Shipley of St. Asaph, a close friend of Benjamin Franklin. By 1779 Bishop Shipley left no doubt about his views in regard to the American revolution when he denounced the British government's policies at a meeting of the Society for the Propagation of the Gospel. At about this time, incidentally, Jones was courting the bishop's daughter, Anna Maria Shipley. His sense of justice would not let him be a mere observer of the American Revolution. He wanted to write "an objective history of the American War."[7] He drew up plans for the history but wanted much reliable information from the American side. Who would be so helpful as Benjamin Franklin whom he met at the Shipley's. Moreover, he now had a client, a certain Mrs. Paradise of Virginia. Franklin could probably arrange for her income from America to reach her in England. Thus, scholarly, professional, and personal friendship drew him in May 1779 to Passy, where Franklin was then living. During the fortnight

[5] *The Catalogue of the Library of Thomas Jefferson,* vol. II, p. 39.
[6] *A Course of Legal Study* (Philadelphia, 1956), p. 46.
[7] Cannon, *Oriental Jones,* p. 57.

he stayed in France, he met Franklin twice and, though neither England nor America asked him to conduct negotiations, he discussed with Franklin the possibilities of reconciliation.

On his return to England, he wrote an allegory, much in the manner of Johnson's accounts of the "Senate of Lilliput." He called it "A Fragment of Polybius", and sent it to his philosopher-friend at Passy on May 28, 1779. Franklin appreciated Jones's efforts to reconcile, at least, the commercial ties of Britain and America. He must have been pleased to find himself referred to as "a philosopher, named Eleutherion, eminent for the deepest knowledge of nature, the most solid judgment, most approved virtue, and most ardent zeal for the cause of general liberty".[8] Franklin told Jones that he perused "A Fragment" with great pleasure but thought that the plan for reconciliation came too late. In this instance we find Jones acting as a self-appointed agent for peace. This same feature of his character was to develop in him the great concern for humanity which he was to show by compiling a digest of laws for the Hindus.

On March 13, 1791, as a circuit court judge for Wales, Jones wrote his famous "Ode in Imitation of Alcaeus," which incidentally resembles William Collins's "Ode to Liberty". Part of the Ode is reproduced here to illustrate the humanist qualities and the distaste for tyranny that Jones consistently maintained which endeared him to American revolutionaries.

What constitutes a state ?
Not high rais'd battlement or labour'd mound,
Thick wall or moated gate;
Not cities proud with spires and turrets crown'd;
Not bays or broad arm'd ports,
Where, laughing at the storm, rich natives ride,
Not star'd and spangled courts,
Where low-bow'd baseness wafts perfume to pride.
No:—Men, high-minded men,
With powers as far above dull brutes endued
In forest, brake, or den,
As beasts, excel cold rocks and brambles rude;
Men, who their duties know,

[8] In the Appendix to *The Works of Benjamin Franklin,* ed. by Jared Sparks (Boston, 1840), vol. VII, pp. 543-547.

But know their rights, and knowing dare maintain,
Prevent the long aim'd blow,
And crush the tyrant while they rend the chain:
These constitute a state,
. . . . [9]

This ode attacked, almost directly, the tyranny of George III and justified revolutions. It made clear where his mind and heart lay. The "Ode" as it turned out was published at a most inopportune moment. He was, at that time, being considered for a judgeship on the bench of the supreme court in India. What if the Princes of India, spurred by the French, should spurn the British and rise in revolt ? Would he protect the British interests, or would he, like the "high minded" idealist he appeared to be, protect human interests and encourage the rebels and invite them to "crush the tyrant?" This ode delayed his appointment in India. But Jones did not care. Instead, he took an active part in the activities of the Society for Constitutional Information to which he was elected as an honorary member in 1782. One of the earliest broadsides of this Society was the *Ode in Imitation of Alcaeus*. In America, this "Ode" became a popular anthology piece. The versatile scholar and editor Robert Walsh included it in "Select Poems of Sir William Jones: with a Life of the Author", in the thirty-fifth volume of his fifty-volume series of *The Works of the British Poets*. The thirty-fifth volume was published in 1822. Robert Walsh was a professor of English at the University of Pennsylvania from 1818 to 1828. He also edited the *Museum of Foreign Literature and Science* from 1822-23 and *The American Quarterly Review* from 1827 to 1837. His *Works of the British Poets* being the first anthology of its kind to be published in America, it is safe to guess that the thirty-fifth volume containing, amongst other poems by Jones, the *Ode in Imitation of Alcaeus* was available to university students in America as early as 1822. In the Library Company of Philadelphia, there is a single sheet broadside of this poem. The library has no history of its accession. It is possible that this broadside is one of many that were in wide circulation before 1822. The same

[9] Robert Walsh, ed., *The Works of the British Poets* (Philadelphia, 1822), vol. XXXV, pp. 109-110.

"Ode" also appears in a bound volume of Political Pamphlets in the Loganian Library in Philadelphia. The pamphlets are related to a controversy between the Old and the New Whigs. Its appearance in this collection is, perhaps, an implied recognition of the philosophy of natural rights the ode seems to espouse and which the American revolutionaries took seriously. The "Ode" seems to have been in the Loganian Library since 1811, judging by the date on its bookplate. It has since been transferred to the Library Company of Philadelphia. In fact Robert Walsh's inclusion of the poems and life sketch of Jones in his multi-volume works of the British poets may be a demonstration of early American recognition of the all-round achievement of Jones. In the twenty-two page "Life of Sir William Jones" which he prefixed to the poems, Walsh refers to Jones with warm admiration for his scholarship and human values.[10]

In the Spring of 1781, Lord Althorp, whom Jones had tutored in 1765-70, married Miss Bingham, the daughter of Lord Lucan. In honor of their marriage, Jones wrote a nuptial ode, "The Muse Recalled". Even in a nuptial ode, he could not refrain from denouncing tyranny and defending freedom:

> Beyond the vast Atlantick deep
> A dome by viewless genii shall be rais'd,
> The walls of adamant compact and steep,
> The portals with sky-tinctur'd gems emblazed:
> There on lofty throne shall Virtue stand;
> To her the youth of Delaware shall kneel;
> And when her smiles rain plenty o'er the land,
> Bow, tyrants bow beneath th'avenging steel![11]

It is difficult to resist the temptation of interpreting his " Muse Recalled" as a prophesy of the affluent America. This optimism, on the other hand, may have been merely a contemporaneous romantic hope in America. All the same it contained another reason why Jones should be held with deep affection and high respect in America. A copy of "The Muse Recalled, an Ode, On the Nuptials of Lord Viscount Althorp and Miss Lavinia

[10] *Ibid.*, pp. 3-24.
[11] A. J. Arberry, *Oriental Essays* (London, 1952), p. 58.

Bingham" can be seen in a bound volume of political pamphlets which once belonged to Benjamin Franklin. These pamphlets were presented to the American Philosophical Society by John Vaughan on October 3, 1828. They are now in the Library Company of Philadelphia. Six major American libraries also acquired copies of this poem prior to 1828.[12] This poem, with its expression of hope for an affluent America, is another instance of Jones's idealism which endeared him to American readers.

In 1782 he realised another long-standing desire to demonstrate his interest in India. This he did by translating Ibn al Mulaqqin's laws of inheritances from Arabic into English as *The Mahomedan Law of Succession to the Property of Intestates.* These laws were meant for application to the Moslems in Bengal. The book was favorably reviewed by Burke, Pitt, and even by King George III and it increased his chances of appointment to the supreme judicature of India.

In June 1782, he found himself in France once again, meeting frequently with Franklin, Lafayette, and Count Charles Vergennes. During one of their conversations, Jones asserted that the basic principles of government could be made intelligible to illiterate people. To prove his point, he wrote a dialogue in French in imitation of one of Plato's. In the seven-page prose dialogue a scholar convinces a peasant that the peasant's club in the village is comparable to a free state. To protect his club from the domination of any single individual is the peasant's right. Thus, in such a simple experience, the peasant learns of his natural right to a voice in the affairs of his government. Franklin seemed convinced. This dialogue was later translated by Jones into English and was published by the Society for Constitutional Information. This was another of Jones's writings to enhance his popularity in America. Without the author's name it was published as *The Principles of Government, in a Dialogue Between a Scholar and a Peasant* (London, 1782). Thomas Jefferson owned a copy.[13]

In October 1782 he proposed to Anna Maria Shipley and she immediately agreed to marry him. His first thoughts were

[12] Jones, *The Muse Recalled, an Ode* . . . (Twickingham, England, 1781).

[13] *Catalogue of the Library of Thomas Jefferson,* vol. III, p. 146.

to inform Franklin to whom he wrote: "My profile will, I hope, have the honour of being hung up in your apartment with those of a family, whom you love and revere, and by whom you are loved and revered with the greatest cordiality. My connection with the excellent Bishop of St. Asaph, by marriage with his eldest daughter (of whom I have heard you speak with approbation) is now settled, and will take place as soon as we can be united with a prudent attention to our worldly interests, and to the highest of all interests, our independence".[14]

The next important event in his life was his appointment on March 4, 1783 to the supreme judicature of India. Now he could realize his dream of exploring Indian literature and legislative and governmental traditions at first hand. He would also be able to reveal to the Europeans the rich lore of the Hindus as he had already helped them to a knowledge of the Persians and Arabs. England had already lost America through what seemed to Jones its stubborn impudence. Could it preserve its Indian Empire by being more level headed? Could it win the trust of India? On Jones rested part of this responsibility and he was more than willing to fulfil his share through his judicial talents and scholarly investigations.

When the news of appointment reached Franklin, he wrote to Jones on March 17, 1783:

You announced your intended marriage with my much respected friend, Miss Anna Maria, which I assure you gave me great pleasure, as I cannot conceive a match more likely to be happy, from the amiable qualities each of you possess so plentifully. You mention its taking place as soon as a prudent attention to wordly interests would permit. I just now learn .... that you are appointed to an honorable and profitable place in the Indies; so I expect now soon to hear of the wedding, and to receive the profile. With the good Bishop's permission, I will join my blessings with his; adding my wishes, that you may return from that corrupting country,

---

[14] Letter dated Nov. 15, 1782 is in the American Philosophical Society Library, Philadelphia, Pa.; also see Garland Cannon, "Sir William Jones and Benjamin Franklin", [Oxford] *University College Record,* IV (Oct. 1961), pp. 27-45, for four previously unpublished letters of Jones to Benjamin Franklin.

with a great deal of money honestly acquired, and with full as much virtue as you carry out with you.[15]

True to his character the old philosopher at Passy was giving timely advice. Such employees of the East India Company as Robert Clive and Warren Hastings had gained a notoriety that has few parallels in the history of imperialism. In the case of Jones, however, Franklin's advice that he "return from that corrupting country, with a great deal of money honestly acquired, and with full as much virtue as you carry out with you" was somewhat superfluous. For, Jones, as he sailed with his wife to India in the *Crocodile* was drawing up a Franklinesque plan of research which he called "Objects of Enquiry During My Residence in Asia". He included sixteen subjects for study which were about Indian law, history, medicine, chemistry, anatomy, trade, manufacturing, agriculture, commerce, geography, arithmetic, geometry, poetry, rhetoric, morality, and music. He was particularly interested in a comparison of Hindu mythology with the Biblical and Classical, to verify such episodes as the Flood. Soon he realized the vastness of the fields of study and it dawned on him that he could start a society for research patterned after the Royal Society. It could reveal Hindu, Moslem, and Chinese cultures to Europe through scholarly researches in archeology, religion, law, philosophy, the arts, and customs of Asian peoples. Besides, the Society could improve relations between the rulers and the ruled and win the trust of the people for the administration.

Once in Calcutta, Jones mentioned his plan about a Society to Sir Robert Chambers, a fellow judge of the supreme court. Chambers applauded the idea and invited a group of learned men to meet in January 1784. Among them was Charles Wilkins who was to become in 1785 the first translator of the *Bhagavad-Gita* into English. The learned men requested Warren Hastings, the then Governor General of India, to be the first president of the Royal Asiatic Society of Bengal. When he declined, Jones was unanimously elected. At their next meeting, he delivered the first Anniversary Discourse. The Anniversary Discourses became a regular feature of the Society establishing

[15] *The Complete Works of Benjamin Franklin*, ed. by John Bigelow (New York, 1888), VIII, pp. 270-271.

a tradition. His first address was entitled "A Discourse on the Institution of a Society for Inquiring into the History, Civil and Natural, the Antiquities, Arts, Sciences and Literature of Asia". In it he proposed a systematic study of an incredible range of subjects and laid down a procedure of research that was hitherto not envisioned by the Orientalists of Europe. The "Discourse" appeared in London the same year (1784) in a thirty-page booklet to which he appended his hymn "To Camdeo," the Hindu god of Love. This publication heightened the expectations of the Europeans with regard to the potential of the Asiatic Society.

Charles Wilkins was now pressing Jones to learn Sanskrit. At the same time a native magistrate mentioned to Jones about a book of Ordinances said to have been revealed by Brahma to Manu, the first man according to Hindu mythology. All of this increased Jones's curiosity about Sanskrit. Hastings had already made this book, *Manava-Dharma-Sastra* (Ordinances of Manu), the basis of Hindu law. But Jones could not even procure a copy of it. Sadly he learnt that Wilkins was not going to translate this very important legal treatise.

Meanwhile time passed, and on the 24th of February 1785, he delivered his Second Anniversary Discourse before the Society. He told the members that they needed to make significant discoveries in history, sciences, and arts so that Indian customs and culture might be better understood in Europe. Once again he referred to the digest of Hindu laws which urgently needed to be compiled. His proposals may have sounded too visionary. But his concern remained undiminished in the subsequent months. He perceived that it was necessary for him to learn Sanskrit in order to stay at the head of *Asiatick Researches*. During the summer of the same year (1785), when he was camping at Krishnagar near Nuddea where there was a Hindu University, he searched for a teacher of Sanskrit. The ideal teacher would be a Brahmin, for the Brahmins have been the traditional custodians of this language and all the learning preserved in it. But no Brahmin was willing to instruct Jones, because Jones, after all, was a beef-eating foreigner. His contact would defile the sacred language and anger the gods. But Jones was not to be discouraged so easily. If a Brahmin would not help, a non-Brahmin would suffice. Thus in the late

Summer of 1785 he found a *Vaidya,* a native medical practitioner, who agreed to be his teacher. They began with a study of Vishnu Sarman's *Hitopadeśa,* a collection of fascinating fables illustrating the art of practical living and upholding *dharma.* *Hitopadeśa* is an excellent example of Hindu "wisdom literature". Beyond this, of course, lay *Manava-dharma-sastra* which was to be translated into English, for that was his objective in learning Sanskrit.

His study of *Hitopadeśa* whetted his appetite and he wrote to his colleague MacPherson, "I would rather be a valetudinarian all my life than leave unexplored the Sanscrit mine which I have just opened".[16] He began putting his Sanskrit learning to use by composing a series of hymns to major Hindu Gods. He read some of them to the Society as examples of Hindu materials in English. Francis Gladwin, the printer of the East India Company at Calcutta, requested his permission to print them in *The Asiatick Miscellany; Consisting of Original Production, Translations, Fugitive Pieces, Imitations, and Extracts from Curious Publications.* Jones readily agreed to such publication and wrote short "Arguments" to each of the hymns in order to help the European reader understand the complex religious and philosophical systems underlying them. The first volume of the *Asiatick Miscellany* appeared in 1785 and instantly brought him wide recognition. An imperfect copy of this two-volume first edition was acquired by the Library Company of Philadelphia before 1800 and a copy in a somewhat better condition was acquired by the Harvard University Library also before 1800. It is not known how and through whom these copies reached these libraries. A subsequent single volume of *Asiatick Miscellany* (1787) was purchased by James Cox, an artist of the city of Philadelphia. There is, however, no evidence indicating Cox's scholarly interest in Sanskrit researches. A bookplate on this copy indicates that Cox purchased it for the Library Company of Philadelphia. No date of purchase is mentioned on the bookplate. Yale University Library, Bryn Mawr College Library, and four other university libraries acquired one copy each of this edition of *Asiatick Miscellany* sometime before 1820. This popularity is evidence of the slow but steadily spreading American interest in Sanskrit literature. An account of

16 Lord Teignmouth, *Memoirs* (Philadelphia, 1805), p. 265.

Emerson's personal interest in *Asiatick Miscellany* and his debt to Jones appears in the last chapter of this dissertation. Benjamin Silliman and Edward Walsh also excerpted Jones's hymns to various Hindu gods from *Asiatick Miscellany* and offered them to American readers during the first three decades of the nineteenth century. A detailed account of this is given in the fourth chapter of this dissertation.

The hymn previously referred to, "A Hymn to Camdeo", was written by Jones in 1784 and was checked by Charles Wilkins. It is the earliest English poem on Hindu mythology accurately portraying the character of Kama, the god of love and the Hindu counterpart of Cupid. Jones succeeded in preserving the sensuous appeal of Kama with his floral arrow-heads, the bow of sugar cane, and the bow-string of bees. It might be said that this poem introduced Hindu romantic imagery for the first time into English poetry:

> WHAT potent God from Agra's Orient bow'rs
> Floats thro' the lucid air, whilst living flow'rs
> With sunny twine, the vocal arbours wreathe,
> And gales enamour'd heav'nly fragrance breathe?
>   Hail, pow'r unknown! for at thy beck
>   Vales and groves their bosoms deck,
>   And ev'ry laughing blossom dresses,
>   With gems of dew his musky tresses,
> I feel, I feel thy genial flame divine,
> And hallow thee and kiss thy shrine.[17]

The next important hymn in this collection is "A Hymn to Narayena". In the first stanza he describes the divine attributes of the Supreme Being and the three mythological personal forms. The most important part of the hymn is, of course, at the end. His ideas came from *Manava-dharma-sastra* which he was then studying:

> First an all-potent, all-pervading sound
>   Bade flow the waters—and the waters flow'd,
>   Exulting in their measureless abode,

[17] *British Poets,* ed. by Robert Walsh (Philadelphia, 1822), XXXV, p. 123.

Diffusive, multitudinous, profound,
   Above, beneath, around;

Then o'er the vast expanse primordial wind
Breath'd gently, till a lucid bubble rose,
Which grew in perfect shape an Egg refin'd:
Created substance no such beauty knows.

And above the warring waves it danced elate,
   Till from its bursting shell with lovely state
   A form cerulean flutter'd o'er the deep,
Brightest of beings, greatest of the great:
     Who, not as mortals steep
     Their eyes in dewy sleep,
But heav'nly-pensive on the Lotos lay,
That blossom'd at his touch and shed a golden ray.[18]

Concealed in this poem is the Vedantic doctrine of creation by emanations. Narayana, the One who dwells on waters, is the Hindu counterpart of the "brooding spirit" of the second verse of the first chapter of the book of *Genesis*.[19] Emerson happened to read this poem at the age of seventeen (1820), at a time when he was trying to express his own ideas about God which were not much different from the monistic ideas of Hinduism and particularly of Vedanta. Emerson's debt to this poem is discussed in the final chapter. Benjamin Silliman, too, excerpts this poem in his *Letters of Shahcoolen* with a view to familiarizing American readers with Vedantic ideas. This is discussed in a later chapter of this dissertation.

The appearance of these hymns in the *Asiatick Miscellany* marked the rising European curiosity in Hindu culture. By 1787 it was reprinted simultaneously in Calcutta and in London. For quite some time this volume was even mistaken for the transactions of Asiatic Society of Bengal. Jones's poems were

[18] *Ibid.*, p. 126.

[19] See *The Interpreters' Bible*. The commentator writes "... the reference to the Spirit 'brooding upon' . . . the chaos has underlying it the idea of a cosmic egg which was hatched by the brooding Spirit, as by a bird, to produce the universe, an idea which is foreign to the story as a whole... it is possible that scribe P was familiar with the Hindu story of Creation in some early form and has squeezed it into the narrative of Genesis".

the central attraction of the first volume.   In them, he had
captured the spirit of the Hindu myths and displayed a rare
insight into Hindu thought.   At the same time he provided
a refreshingly new imagery, different even from that of the
Arabic and Persian literatures.   And his early American readers
did not miss this freshness.

Prior to the Sanskrit studies of Jones, there was in Europe
a faint recognition of the affinity of Sanskrit with Greek and
Latin.   Fillippo Sassetti in 1585, Benjamin Schultze in 1725,
and Father Cordoux in 1767 had suggested this affinity.   But
their suggestions were soon swept away into the unscientific
theories of the time.   It was thought that Latin came from
Greek, and that Greek came from Sanskrit.[21]   Jones, like
many European scholars, was well grounded in Greek and
Latin and in addition knew several Germanic languages. Therefore, when he came across a precise statement of Sanskrit
grammar or a careful analysis of a lexical form in Panini's text
(5th century B.C.) he could recognize the cognate phonetic
and structural resemblances with Greek and Latin and to him
this indicated a probable parallel development of all the three
classical languages.   Thus in the Third Anniversary Discourse
of February 2, 1786, he presented his theory:

> The *Sanscrit* language, whatever be its antiquity, is of a
> wonderful structure; more perfect than Greek, more copious
> than *Latin,* and more exquisitely refined than either, yet
> bearing to both of them a stronger affinity, both in the roots
> of verbs and in the forms of grammar, than could possibly
> have sprung from some common source, which, perhaps,
> no longer exists; there is a similar reason, though not quite
> forcible, for supposing that both *Gothick* and *Celtick,* though
> blended with very different idiom, had the same origin with
> the Sanscrit; and the old *Persian* might he added to the
> same family.[22]

In these words, he became the first linguist to propound the
theory of Indo-Germanic family of languages with the possibility
of their having derived from a hypothetical ancestor.   These

[21] Cannon, *Oriental Jones,* p. 139.
[22] Jones, *Works,* I (London, 1799), p. 26, hereafter Jones, *Works.*

were the historic words that initiated the science of comparative philology. Almost every textbook on the history of language quotes this passage.[23] The German and French philologists who conducted a scientific study of comparative linguistics, found Jones's hypothesis correct. As has been suggested in this dissertation, American interest in Sanskrit studies, however, was behind European interest by at least four decades. An examination of the published and unpublished papers of Noah Webster at the New York Public Library does not give any evidence of Webster's knowledge of Jones's theory of a common ancestry of Sanskrit, Latin, Greek, Gothic, and Celtic.

After this famous speech, despite the illness of both his wife and himself, Jones started a translation of the *Ordinances of Manu* (Manava-dharma-sastra).[24] This was the necessary first step to the compilation of a digest of Hindu laws which would assure the welfare of the Indian subjects. At the same time he was editing the first volume of *Asiatick Researches* consisting of the weekly papers read in the Society. Many of those papers were his own and he had to edit the rest of the submissions himself. In the midst of all these preoccupations he was still studying *Hitopadeśa*. This was the text he read in order to learn Sanskrit and to improve his facility in that language. And even as he progressed in reading, he translated the text. Thus in the middle of 1786, Jones brought out the first English translation of *Hitopadeśa*.[25]

Towards the end of 1788 Jones had mastered Sanskrit more completely than he had mastered any other language. He was now officially supervising the translation of *Manava-dharma-sastra*. The East India Company came forward with financial support for the project. Meanwhile, he continued to make much progress in editing the *Asiatick Researches,* the first volume of which was published in 1789. The very first selection in it, in fact, was his own paper, "A Dissertation on the Orthography of Asiatick Words in Roman Letters". In it, he offered a systematic method of transliterating Sanskrit, Persian, and Arabic. This

[23] Leonard Bloomfield, *Language* (New York, 1966), p. 12.

[24] *Institutes of Hindu Law; Or, the Ordinances of Menu, According to the Gloss of Culluca* .... Calcutta; By Order of the Govt., 1794.

[25] Franklin Edgerton, "Sir William Jones: 1745-1794", *JAOS,* LXVI (July 1946), p. 232.

system may be described as the earliest attempt at formulating
an International Phonetic Alphabet for at least four languages.[26]
    Another important research paper that Jones published in the
first volume of *Asiatick Researches* is "On the Gods of Greece,
Italy, and India". In it he presented a thesis that stimulated
the curiosity of many European theologians and anthropologists.
Briefly, it is as follows:

> When features of resemblance, too strong to have been
> accidental, are observed in different systems of polytheism,
> without fancy or prejudice to color them and improve the
> likeness, we can scarce help believing, that some connection
> has immemorially subsisted between the several nations, who
> have adopted them.[27]

In these words he became the first Westener to recognize a
common cultural origin of the Indo-European and at the same
time laid the foundations of comparative religions. Emerson's
readiness to write a poem entitled "Brahma" may have been
the result of Jones's researches into the resemblances between
the mythologies of Greece, Italy, and India. More of this is
discussed in the final chapter of this book.
    One more essay which suggests Jones's mission and achieve-
ment is his paper "On the Literature of the Hindus, from the
Sanscrit". In this essay he gave an account of the extant
Sanskrit books, and discussed the several parts of Hindu literature,
law, the six systems of philosophy, and Buddhist writings. His
sense of fairplay led him to comment that Britain should give
an accurate account of Hindu religion and literature to the
Western world.
    Jones's translation of Jayadeva's *Gitagovinda* marked his incur-
sion into major Sanskrit literature. Early in 1789, he made a
literal translation of this exotic poem, sacrificing the lyric qualities
of the original. This work was included in the third volume
of the *Asiatick Researches*. He may have thought *Gitagovinda*
the supreme example of the Hindu literature because it combines
philosophy, mysticism, eroticism, and artistic expression. He
prefaced it with a nineteen-page dissertation "On the Mystical
Poetry of the Persians and Hindus" in which he explained:

[26] I, pp. 1-56.   [27] Cannon, *Oriental Jones*, p. 157.

.... the loves of CRISHNA and RADHA, or the reciprocal attraction between the divine goodness and the human soul, are told at large in the tenth book of *Bhagavat,* and are the subject of a little *Pastoral Drama* entitled *Gitagovinda.* It was the work of JAYADEVA, who flourished, it is said, before CALIDAS....[28]

Jones, of course, bowdlerized this poem by "omitting only those passages, which are too luxuriant and too bold for an *European* taste".[29]

By now the Brahmins themselves had discovered, and were impressed by, Jones's scholarly sincerity and humanistic concerns. They now came forward to help him with the translation of *The Ordinances of Manu.* It mattered to them no longer that he was a foreigner. They conversed with him in Sanskrit and were willing to show him their sacred literature. One of them had told him of a set of ancient books called *natakas.* They were dramas, many in number, the best of which was Kalidas's *Śakuntala.* The Indian masses were not aware of this literature. Only the Brahmins knew about it. Jones was excited about the prospect of restoring forgotten literature to the masses in India and at the same time informing Europeans about them. He translated *Śakuntala* line by line first into Latin and then into English. As a keen judge of literature, he knew that he had uncovered an example of drama that would stand amongst the world's greatest. When he completed it in October 1789, he published it immediately in Calcutta with the title, *Śacontala; or the Fatal Ring: an Indian Drama.* In his preface he called the Indian playwright Kalidasa, the Shakespeare of India. When *Śacontala* reached Europe it caused more excitement than any other Oriental translation. Within seven years it was reprinted thrice in Great Britain and was translated into German, French, and Italian.[30] In America, Thomas Jefferson owned a copy of the 1790 reprint of this drama. He must have acquired it in 1791, for, in that year we find him writing to his book agent Benjamin Vaughn, "I thank you, my dear friend, for the

---

[28] *Asiatick Researches,* III (London, 1792), pp. 182-183.
[29] *Loc. cit.*
[30] Cannon, *Oriental Jones,* p. 165.

Sacontala...."[31] A London 1792 edition of this drama seems
to have reached a wider circle of American readers.   Copies
of this later edition are still to be found in the Library Company
of Philadelphia, Harvard University Library, and Cleveland
Public Library.   Besides, this drama was also available to
American readers in the Sixth Volume of Jones's *Works* (pp.
201-312), which was available at many more libraries.   In
India itself, the translation and publication of *Sacontala* preci-
pitated a literary rebirth.   Sanskrit literature no longer remained
secret.   All the literate Indians began to take just pride in
their long forgotten literary heritage.   This rejuvenation was
the beginning too of the Indian literary Renaissance.[32]

After the universal acclaim that his *Sacontala* received, Jones
decided that Indians should have an opportunity to know their
own literature better.   So he chose to translate *Ṛtusamhara,*
a lyric poem attributed to Kalidasa.   He came across four
different versions of it which he studied closely before bringing
out in 1792 a collated version in Sanskrit, to which he added
an English preface.   This made him the first European editor
of a Sanskrit work.

Next, as a result of his labors in the projected digest of Hindu
laws, the *Institutes of Hindu Law: or, the Ordinances of Menu,
according to the Gloss of Culluca, comprising the Indian System
of Duties, Religious and Civil* was published early in 1794 at
Calcutta.   His "Preface" is an example of the finest prose of the
eighteenth century:

> The work, now presented to the *European* world, contains
> abundance of curious matter extremely interesting both to
> speculative lawyers and antiquaries, with many beauties,
> which need not be pointed out, and with many blemishes,
> which cannot be justified or palliated.   It is a system of
> despotism and priestcraft, both indeed limited by law, but
> artfully conspiring to give mutual support, though with mutual
> checks; it is filled with strange conceits in metapysicks and
> natural philosophy, with idle superstitions, and with a scheme

[31] *A Catalogue of the Library of Thomas Jefferson* (Washington:
Library of Congress), Vol. IV, p. 488.

[32] K. R. S. Iyenger, *The Indian Contribution to English Literature*
(Bombay, 1945), p. 2.

of theology most obscuredly figurative, and consequently liable to dangerous misconception; it abounds with minute and childish formalities, with ceremonies generally absurd and often ridiculous; the punishments are partial and fanciful, for some crimes on the whole, are in one or two instances (as in the case of light oaths and of pious perjury) unaccountably relaxed; nevertheless, a spirit of sublime devotion, of benevolence to mankind, and of amiable tenderness to all sentient creatures, pervades the whole work; the style of it has a certain austere majesty, that sounds like the language of legislation and harsh admonitions even to kings are truly noble. . . . It must be remembered, that those laws are actually revered, as the word of the Most High, by nations, of great importance to the political and commercial interests of *Europe,* and particularly by many millions of Hindu subjects. . . . [33]

While the compilation of the "Digest" was in progress, the public acclaim brought by *The Ordinances of Menu* spurred him on to make new plans of research in Sanskrit literature. In his eleventh "Discourse" to the Society, on February 20, 1794, he dealt with the metaphysics, ethics, and religion of the Vedas with which he now showed admirable familiarity.

He was hoping to retire soon after the compilation of the "Digest". Ill health had already forced his wife to return to England. He was going to join her and, during their retirement, intended to apply himself to more researches in Sanskrit. So he drew up a plan under the title of "desiderata". Among other things, he wanted to write a Sanskrit grammar, a dictionary, a history of pre-Islamic India, and translations of the *Vedas, Mahabharata,* and *Ramayana.*[34]

By April 1794, he completed his editorial work on the fourth volume of the *Asiatick Researches.* The first four volumes enhanced his reputation as an Orientalist and linguist enormously. Selections from the first three volumes of the *Asiatick Researches* and the *Asiatick Miscellany* had been published first in London and then in Dublin in two volumes in 1792 and 1793 respectively under the title of *Dissertations and Miscellaneous Pieces* in

[33] Jones, *Works,* III, pp. 61-63.
[34] Cannon, *Oriental Jones,* p. 181.

which half the selections were taken from Jones's writings. Within a decade thirteen major American Universities and Colleges acquired copies of these two volumes. Heedless of the gathering international applause, Jones continued to work on the "Digest".[35] Of the pain from an inflamed liver, he complained little. And he would not think of returning to England before the completion of the "Digest".

Unfortunately, the tropical climate of Bengal had already wrought its harm on Jones. His sickness became acute until, on the 27th of April, 1794, after a day of delirium, he passed away peacefully on his couch. Thus, at the age of forty-eight came to an end the life of a man who sought to harmonize jurisprudence and individual independence, administrative professionalism and scholarly excellence, and East and West. His example is often praised but seldom followed. In India, he had initiated a renaissance of national culture. In America, his universal humanity was personally recognized by Benjamin Franklin who wished Jones well both in person and by letter. Indeed, his love of liberty and humanitarianism and particularly his use of jurisprudence in the service of man was readily acknowledged in America as early as 1805. The craving for an account of the life and works of this remarkable man caused William Poyntell and Company of Philadelphia to bring out in 1805 the first American edition of Lord Teignmouth's *Memoirs of the Life, Writings and Correspondence of Sir William Jones.*[36]

As a result of the rising American interest in the life and works of Jones, Robert Walsh admiringly included Jones's Hindu poems as early as 1822 in his multivolume anthology of British poets. Besides, Jones's "Ode in Imitation of Alcaeus" had been popular because of its vehement defence of America's liberty

---

[35] For an account of the influence of Jones on English Literature, see Marie E. de Meester, *Oriental Influence in the English Literature of the Nineteenth Century* (Heidelberg, 1915); Vincent de Sola Pinto, "Sir William Jones and English Literature," *Bulletin of the School of Oriental and African Studies,* XI, 4 (1946), pp. 685-694.

[36] Needless to say that the first American edition of the biography of Jones found its way into every major College and private library in North America during the first decade of the 19th century, thus rousing the curiosity of the American public about the writings of Jones and his English translations of Sanskrit literature much of which contained Vedantic ideas.

and it was known both to Benjamin Franklin and Thomas Jefferson. The Library Company of Philadelphia has a single sheet broadside copy of this "Ode". A similar broadside also appears in a bound volume of a set of Political Pamphlets in the Loganian Library. These Pamphlets are related to a controversy between the Old and the New Whigs. Its appearance in this collection is a sure sign of recognition of the philosophy of natural rights this "Ode" espouses. The "Ode" along with the Political Pamphlets has been in the Loganian Library since 1811 according to the date on the bookplate. This collection of Pamphlets has since been transferred to the Library Company of Philadelphia. Franklin and Jefferson were certainly aware of these Pamphlets.

In fact, Jones's translation of the Sanskrit play *Sacontala* was owned by Thomas Jefferson as has been pointed out earlier in this chapter. He referred to the play appreciatively enough to suggest that he was proud of possessing it. Jefferson also owned a copy of Jones's dialogue on *The Principles of Government* and he, like Jones, believed that such principles could be taught to any person, literate or illiterate.

Early American interest in Vedic literature and Vedantic philosophy is typified by Jefferson's interest in Jones as a jurist, a defender of human liberty, and, finally, a translator of Sanskrit literature. It is true that Jefferson did not express himself enthusiastically over Vedic literature and Vedantic philosophy as did Emerson decades later. Nevertheless, Jefferson's interest should be recognized, even if it is a passing kind of interest. As against Jefferson's, Robert Walsh's inclusion of Jones's Hymns to "Camdeo" and "Narayena" in his edition of British Poets must be noted as an example of the scholarly early American interest in Vedic literature and Vedantic philosophy.

Humanitarian motives like love of liberty and universal human dignity first impelled Jones to sympathize with American political independence from Britain. His sympathies moved him to write a poem and a dialogue in praise of freedom and democratic government. Those writings became favorite anthology pieces and prized collector's items in America and endeared him to the American literate public. Then, similar motives took him to India where he established the Asiatic

Society of Bengal through which he published many discoveries of Vedic literature and Vedantic philosophy, and Hindu law in English translations. The American literati kept track of his writings. Thus, out of admiration for the career of a political sympathizer and mentor in Common Law, came America's opportunity for a contact with Vedic literature and Vedantic philosophy. His life and works initiated a systematic probe into the wealth of Vedic literature and Vedantic philosophy. America and Europe have benefited from his pioneering works. In subsequent years American scholars shared British and European curiosity in Vedic literature and Vedantic philosophy. This shall be our subject in the chapters that follow.

4

OTHER WORKS ON VEDIC LITERATURE AND VEDANTIC PHILOSOPHY AVAILABLE IN AMERICA BEFORE 1840

THE COLONIAL rivalry of the French and the English during the eighteenth century, showed itself sometimes in the field of scholarship as well. At the time Sir William Jones in England was occupied in Arabic and Persian researches, Abraham Hyacinthe Anquetil-Duperron[1] had already earned a modest reputation in France as a scholar in Arabic and Persian.

Born a decade and a half earlier than Jones, he had the advantage of an earlier start. From an interest in Hebrew he realized the need to master Arabic, Chaldaic, and Persian. His linguistic reputation soon reached the ears of Bishop M. de Caylus of Auxerre, who invited him to his academy in order to prepare for an ecclesiastical vocation. After some time at Auxerre, he proceeded to Amersfoort near Utrecht where he improved his knowledge of Arabic and Persian. When he was convinced that he had learned all that could be learned at Amersfoort, he returned to Paris. The usual allurements of a comfortable church life and the possibility of an illustrious diplomatic career in an age of French colonial expansion did not tempt him. His inclinations lay in exploring the hidden riches of Arabic and Persian literatures. At Paris he spent all his time at the Royal Library. There, his diligent labors attracted the attention of the Abbé Sallier, the keeper of the manuscripts. Sallier introduced him to his friends and with their influence secured for him a remunerative position as a research scholar

---

[1] J. J. Modi's "Anquetil-Duperron of Pari-India as Seen by Him", *Journal of the Bombay Branch of the Royal Asiatic Society,* XXIV (1917), pp. 313-456; also see *Biographie Universelle (Michaud): Ancienne et Moderne,* (Paris: Nouvelle Edition, n.d.).

in Oriental languages. During this time he came across some
Persian manuscripts in Zend characters. This script is different
from modern Persian which is influenced linguistically by
Aramaic. To decipher these manuscripts, he had to meet
Zoroastrians who had fled from Persia and settled in India.
So impatient was he to decipher these Zend characters that he
signed up as a common soldier with a French expedition to
India. When his friends heard of this hasty behavior, they
approached the Minister. On hearing this story of uncommon
scholarly impatience, the Minister ordered that Duperron be
given a free passage and a seat at the Captain's table. Thus
provided, he landed in the French-Indian port of Pondicherry on
August 10, 1775. At Pondicherry, he improved his familiarity
with modern Persian. But still not satisfied, he wanted to
learn Sanskrit as well and went to Chandranagoor, which was
another French-Indian port. Here he was greatly disappointed
in that he found nobody who was willing to teach him Sanskrit.
Besides, he was sick for many months. Meanwhile the French-
British rivalry in India errupted into open war. Chandranagoor
was taken by the British in 1757 and Duperron was forced
to flee incognito. Despite incredible hardships, he trudged
through four hundred leagues in about a hundred days and
returned to Pondicherry on foot. From there he traveled by
sea and land and reached Surat where there were many Parsees.
At Surat he was able to procure from the Zoroastrian priests
more Persian manuscripts, one of which was *Vendidade Sade,*
a dictionary which he translated into French. It was also at
this place that he secured the Persian translation of *Oupnek'hat*
which he was to translate later into Latin. The *Oupnek'hat*
must have heightened his desire to master Sanskrit, which he
thought he could do at Benares. But just then he was obliged
to give himself up to the British, who treated him graciously
and took him in one of their ships to London. Then he visited
Oxford, where he was allowed to examine some Arabic and
Persian manuscripts at the Bodleian. At last on May 4, 1762,
he returned to Paris to spend the rest of his life in editing some
of the 180 manuscripts he had acquired and which he now
deposited in the Royal Library.

After much arduous work, in 1771, he published the *Zend
Avesta, Ouvrage de Zoroastre* in three volumes. In his

prefatory account of his Indian adventures, he boasted of his scholarship but referred to the British scholars as brutes. This outraged Sir William Jones, who in 1771 was a student of law and had already published *The Life of Nadir Shah* and a *Persian Grammar*. In the same preface Duperron also promised that he would later publish a translation of the sacred literature of the Brahmins. To Jones this sounded like another of Duperron's characteristic rantings. Jones's reaction was a fifty-page *Lettre a Monsieur A*** du P**** (1771).[2] Seven years later, Duperron published his *Legislation Orientale* (1778).[3] Here he gave an account of the fundamental principles of government in the Turkish, Persian, and Indian dominions. He proved that the legendary "Oriental despotism" was not absolute and that there are codes of written law which affected the prince as well as the subject, and that the inhabitants of the three empires possessed both movable and immovable property and enjoyed liberty. In 1786 he published his *Recherches Historiques et Geographiques sur l'Inde*. It contains much fable and myth, but, it was the first European attempt at reconstructing the historical past of India.

During the Revolution in 1792 Duperron seems to have concealed himself in the library amongst his books. In 1798 he brought out his *L'Indes au Rapport avec l'Europe* in two volumes. This is a commercial treatise on the advantages of promoting European trade with India. It indicates another instance of Western interest in India.

It was not till 1801, however, that he published the first volume of *Oupnek'hat, id est, Secretum Tegendum* with the explanatory subtitle; *Opus ipsa in India rarissimum, continens antiquam et arcanum, seu Theologicam et Philosophicam Doctrinam è quator sacris Indorum libris, Rak Beid, Djedjr Beid, Sam Beid, Atharban Beid, excerptam; Adverbum, é Persico idiomate, Sanskriticis vocabulis intermixto, in Latinum Conversum; Dissertationibus et Annotationibus, difficiliora explanantibus, illustratum: Studio et Opera Anquetil-Duperron.*[4] The second volume was published the following year.

---

[2] A detailed account of the controversy is given by Cannon in *Oriental Jones*, pp. 25-27.

[3] Published in Amsterdam by M. M. Ray.

[4] (Paris: Lavrault, 1801).

In a note on the Persian translation Duperron narrates the history of the manuscript. It is a collection of fifty *Upaniṣads* translated from Sanskrit into Persian under the direction of the Mughul prince Dara Shakoh, the eldest son of Emperor Shah Jehan.[5] The selections were not all *Upaniṣads*. Some of them were *Brahmaṇas* which, along with the *Upaniṣads,* were appended to the four *Vedas*. The distinction between the *Upaniṣads* and the *Brahmaṇas* was often lost to early scholars. The Persian translation was produced in the seventeenth century, though Duperron wrongly states that it was brought out in 1050. During the seventeenth century Persian had replaced Sanskrit as the language of the Indian courts. Either the cooperation of the native Sanskrit scholars may not have been entirely sincere because of the belief in the sacredness of Upaniṣadic lore; or, perhaps the Persian scholars Persianized most Sanskrit terms. The result is that most of the Sanskrit terms were rendered into Persian beyond easy recognition now. *Veda,* for instance has become *Beid* even in Duperron's Latin translation and *Upaniṣad* has become *Oupnek'hat.*[6]

Despite these linguistic aberrations, *Oupnek'hat* contained concepts, doctrines, philosophy and religion that are literally Vedantic. Duperron also attempted to give a systematic exposition of the Vedantic teachings. His own early preparation for a church vocation and his later linguistic and literary pursuits eminently qualified him both to translate, explicate and compare the "theology" of the *Vedas* with that of Western systematic Christian theology. He had already commented on the theology of *Zend Avesta*. He was now in a position to comment on the similarities and dissimilarities between the Christian, Zoroastrian, and Hindu "theologies". His investigations appear in four well composed dissertations, in *qua é Judeorum, et tam catholicorum quam acatholicorum theologorum scriptis summa Orientalis systematic inquiritur.*[7] Many of his opinions might now seem naïve. He was comparing Vedanta which is essentially the foundation of six systems of Hindu philosophies, to the theologically rigid and doctrinaire religion of Christianity. But, at the

---

[5] *A Dictionary of Indian History* compiled by Sachchidananda Bhattacharya (Calcutta, 1967).

[6] I, p. 6.

[7] *Ibid.,* I, p. **xxiv**.

same time, Duperron introduced terms like *Brahman* and *Ātman;* he sensed that there were two schools of Vedanta, i.e., *dvaita* and *advaita;* he discussed the concept of *Māya* and the doctrine of creation through emanation; and he even commented on the similarities between some aspects of Kant's philosophy and those of Vedanta.[8]

Clearly, Duperron intended his work to be read by serious philosophers and theologians. This might be the reason behind his translating it into Latin. His efforts were noticed first in Germany. Schopenhauer and Schelling read this translation and expressed their enthusiasm in admiring terms. Schopenhauer in particular said that the *Upaniṣads* are "the production of the highest human wisdom".[9] One might say that Schopenhauer set a fashion of enthusiastic admiration for Vedantic philosophy. When we come to Emerson and Thoreau's reactions it is no wonder that we find them as enthusiastic about Vedanta as was Schopenhauer. Six years after its publication in Paris, Thaddae Anselm Rixner, a professor of Philosophy brought out an abridged German translation entitled, *Versuch einer neuen Darstellung der uralten indischen All-Eins-Lehre.*[10]

The British scholars did not receive *Oupnek'hat* as enthusiastically as did the Germans. In fact, they ignored it, preferring to wait for their own scholars to come up with authentic English translations. Nevertheless, the *Oupnek'hat* crossed the Atlantic and made its passage to English-speaking America where it was studied in several divinity schools.

Until the appearance of *Oupnek'hat* textbooks of philosophy published in Europe and America were confined almost entirely to an account of European philosophy. The few references to the philosophies of India were derived from what little was reported by Megasthenes, Arrian, and Plutarch. Now the whole range of information had suddenly broadened and the philosophy textbooks after 1802 began to include Vedantic philosophy. In connection with this, mention must be made especially of Joseph Marie Degerando's *Histoire Comparee de Systemes de Philosophie,*[11] a book published in 1804 a little before the

---

[8] *Ibid.,* II, pp. 711-724.

[9] Moriz Winternitz, *A History of Indian Literature* (Calcutta, 1959), I, p. 17.

[10] (Nurnberg, 1808).   [11] 4 vols. (Paris, 1804).

quiet demise of Duperron. Degerando's work reached the
United States almost as soon as it was published and was popular
on the campuses. It became the standard textbook on philosophy.
Its American reception is dealt with at length in the following
chapter. In it, one could read about the pioneering scholarship
of Duperron in discovering Vedanta. Degerando also admiringly
refers to Duperron's "large number of annotations and several
dissertations on the philosophical systems of ancients and
moderns".[12] Besides quoting from *Oupnek'hat,* he discussed the
doctrine of emanations as found among the Egyptians,
Phoenicians, Chaldeeans, Zoroastrians, and Hindus. He remarks
that the doctrine of emanations is "the foundation of the
doctrines of Indians".[13] Related to this doctrine are the doctrines
of Immanence, Compensation, *Māya,* and Metempsychosis.
Emerson, who read Degerando, may have discovered this connection which seems to be the foundation of his own philosophy
of identity.[14] Emerson borrowed volumes I and II from Boston
Athenaeum on Jan. 1, 1830 and volume IV on Feb. 1, 1830.[15]
In addition, Sir William Jones had already referred to the
doctrine of emanations in his preface to "A Hymn to Narayena".
Emerson was first informed of it by his aunt Mary Moody
Emerson.[16]

Degerando was therefore an important link in introducing
Vedantic philosophy to American intellectuals. That he was
well known in the United States is evident by the fact that a
two-volume work of his, *Du Perfectionement Moral, ou De
l'Education de Soi-Meme,* was translated into English and
published in Boston as early as 1832.[17] It contains many ideas
which anticipate Emerson's ideas in his lecture on *Self-Reliance.*
Through Degerando many more American thinkers besides
Emerson must have become acquainted with Vedanta.

Another Frenchman who wrote about India in general is the

---

12 *Ibid.* (2nd edn., 1822), p. 139.   13 *Loc. cit.*

14 See Emerson's *Journals,* II, p. 333.   15 Carpenter, p. 278.

16 *The Journals and Miscellaneous Notes of Ralph Waldo Emerson,*
ed. by William H. Gilman, *et al.* (Cambridge, Mass., 1960), I. p. 154,
f.n. 69, hereafter cited as Emerson, *JMN.*

17 The original was published in Paris by Antoine-Augustine Renouard,
1824.

Abbé J. A. Dubois.[18]   He went to India primarily as a Christian missionary.   But soon he found that he would have to educate himself thoroughly in the philosophies and literature of India. He became a member of the Asiatic Society of Paris, the Asiatic Society of Great Britain, and the Literary Society of Madras. Leaving Paris at the beginning of the Revolution, he settled in Mysore, where he hoped to make a start in evangelizing India. He lived there for thirty-two years and acquired an intimate knowledge of the manners, customs and religious beliefs of the Hindus.   His experience taught him that it was well-nigh impossible to convert the Hindus from a religion that they had practiced for many centuries.   He described his futile evangelistic attempts and noted his observations in a manuscript which was bought by the East India Company of Great Britain and published in English as a *Description of the Character, Manners, and Customs of the People of India, and their Institutions, Religious and Civil.*[19]   Published in 1817, it understandably became very popular among the British officers of India.   The officers were eager not to offend the religious and cultural sensibilities of the Hindus because their success in establishing the British empire depended largely in winning their trust.   The same work also became popular with another class of Englishmen, the British missionaries.   About this time, in America, too, there was a growing missionary interest in India.   In America the sense of evangelistic urgency seems to have been stronger than in England, a fact which seems to have prompted the publication of Dubois' work in Philadelphia in 1818 a year after its publication in London.[20]   This testifies to deep American interest in India as early as the second decade of the nineteenth century.   Though this interest began as exclusively evangelistic, within a short time it led American readers to information on India that contained excerpts from Vedic literature and ideas from Vedantic philosophy.

In the first volume of Dubois' work an American reader could find a whole chapter on the subject "Of the Literature of the Brahmins and Particularly their Poetry".   Dubois has

[18] In the absence of an adequate biography of the Abbe J. A. Dubois, I have gathered this information from *Biographie Universaille* (*Michaud*), Paris, n.d.

[19] 2 vols. (London, 1817).   [20] M. Carey & Son.

illustrated in great detail several important points of Sanskrit poetics such as the measures used in versification [*chchandas*], the internal rhymes [*yati*], the figures of speech, and the quality of Hindu imagination.[21]

In the second volume the American reader could find a summary of the "Opinions of the Hindu Philosophers on the Nature of God, of the Different Beings in the Universe, and Particularly the Soul".[22] The following passage contains a lucid exposition of Vedantic ideas.

> "God", to use the words of the philosophers of India, "is an immaterial Being, pure and unmixed, without qualities, form or division; the Lord and Master of all things. He extends over all, sees all, knows all; without beginning, and without end. Power, strength, and gladness dwell with Him".
>
> This is but a slight sketch of the lofty terms in which the Hindu writings, after their philosophers, describe the Para-Brahma or Supreme Being. But it is painful to see these sublime attributes unworthily profaned, by prostituting them with innumerable other attributes, as ridiculous and absurd as the fables to which they are attached.[23]

Like Duperron, Dubois acquaints the reader with the two schools of Vedanta, the "first called *Dvitam*" and "the other sect is called *Advaitam*".[24] *Māya*, he explains through a story and relates it to the Vedantic principle *"abhavana bhava-nasti*: from nothing nothing comes". He elaborates it in the following words:

> They [the *advaitins*] maintain that *Creation* is an impossibility, and that, on the other hand, a pre-existing and eternal substance is absolutely chimerical. From these premises they infer, that, whatever we imagine to be the universe, and the various objects which appear to compose it, is nothing but a pure illusion, or *Maya* . . . . that which we take for reality is nothing more than a deception from Deity, the only being that exists; and the various things we behold are but appearances, or rather modifications of the Divinity.[25]

[21] *Ibid.*, pp. 353-367.　　[22] *Ibid.*, pp. 56-64.
[23] *Ibid.*, pp. 56-57.
[24] *Ibid.*, p. 57.　　[25] *Ibid.*, pp. 57-58.

As one can see, the above assessment is fair and agrees with the definition of *Māya* given in the first chapter of this dissertation.[26] What is more, Dubois goes beyond a discussion of the two schools of Vedanta and explains "another scheme of philosophy . . . which is followed and taught by the Jains and the votaries of Buddha". In his words, "This system is nothing else than the pure *Materialism,* which Spinoza and his disciples have endeavored to pass for a new discovery of their own. The materialists of India appear to have long preceded them in this doctrine, and have drawn from it the same practical deductions which their European brethren have done, and which have been propagated in modern times with such pernicious success".[27]

On another page Dubois strikes closer to the heart of Vedanta:

The doctrine of the Ascetic philosophers was, that Retirement should dissipate the clouds of Illusion which leads us astray, and break the chains which unite us too closely with the created beings that surround us; as well as with our own evil passions, which entangle, depress, and pollute the soul. Being thus set free, it rejoins the Divinity, even Para-Brahma; and the penitent, now cleansed from the stains of guilt which defiled other men, can boldly exclaim, "Behold a Brahman! I am wholly divine: I am Brahman!"[28]

He comments too on the possibilities of such an outlook leading to the making of the Brahmanical Superman: "Men, whom vain philosophy had beguiled into this ecstatical pride, cannot fail to look upon all other mortals with contempt; as wretches whose accumulated pollution and sins require the revolution of generations to expiate".[29]

Though much of the space in these two volumes of Dubois is devoted to a description of the religious customs, social organization, mythology, fables, chronology, and military organization of the Hindus, any reader could have gained a preliminary insight into the Vedantic concepts of *Brahman, Māya* and their major role in the religious life and popular attitudes of

[26] P. 20 of this book.
[27] *Op. cit.,* p. 59. [28] *Ibid.,* 65. [29] *Loc. cit.*

the Hindus.   There are also oblique references to the four
Vedas and somewhat direct references to numerous *Puraṇas*.
Unfortunately, Dubois has not given us the exact source of his
extracts.   But his narratives are so readable that on that count
alone his two-volume work was popular enough in America
to warrant an American edition in 1818.   Even if one read
these two volumes out of an evangelistic curiosity in India, one
could not have escaped the obvious description of Vedic literature
and Vedantic philosophy.   Later, in 1826, Dubois published
in Paris a Sanskrit-French translation, *Le Pantcha-tantra, ou, les
Cinq Ruses, fables du Brahme Vichnou-Sarman.*[30]   This work
had no missionary appeal and, perhaps, for that reason failed
to capture the imagination of American publishers and readers.
It was not even reviewed in America.

Another French scholar whose works familiarized American
readers with Vedic literature is Alexander Langlois.   He took
up Sanskrit studies under the guidance of Eugene Burnouf and
Abel Remusat.   In 1824 he read a treatise at the general meeting
of the Asiatic Society of Paris.   In it he summarized the passage
of Vedantic ideas into Greek literature and philosophy after
1000 B.C.   In 1827 he took up the same subject in a separate
volume entitled *Literary Monuments of India; or, A Collection
of Sanskrit Literature.*   It contained several selections which
were translated for the first time from Sanskrit into French.
Notable among them was his translation of a semi-epic poem,
"Harivansa, or the History of the Family of Hari", which is an
extension of the epic *Mahabharata*.   His *Harivansa* was separately
published in French in London in 1834 by the Oriental Translation Fund, the two volumes totalling 1147 pages.   Thoreau
borrowed these volumes from the Harvard College Library on
April 24, 1850.[31]   Thoreau translated a portion of this work
as *The Transmigration of Seven Brahmins.*[32]   Langlois went
on to publish in 1828 his *Masterpieces of Indian Theatre* which
was so popular in France that it became a conversational piece
for a time.   At the same time it also raised French curiosity about
Indian literary and philosophical heritage so that Langlois sub-

---

[30] Subtitled *Aventure de Paramartha, et autres Contes, le tout traduit
pour le premier fois sur le originaux indiens;* published by J. S. Merlin.
[31] Thoreau, *Journals,* II, pp. 190-191.
[32] Not published till 1931.

sequently published his four-volume translation of *The Rigveda* from 1848 to 1851.[33]

Thus the French researches in Vedic literature and Vedantic philosophy starting with Anquetil-Duperron were furthered by the efforts of Degerando, Dubois, and Langlois. As we have seen, most of their works were available in America before 1840. Such books were not in the mainstream of American reading, but they certainly contributed to intensifying American interest in Vedic literature and Vedantic philosophy.

While the French vied with the British in Sanskrit scholarship, the latter continued the tradition of Sir William Jones. The *Asiatick Researches* continued to publish more discoveries and thus encouraged the English-speaking peoples to maintain and enhance their interest in Vedic literature and Vedantic philosophy.

One of those who helped Jones in founding the Asiatic Society of Bengal was Charles Wilkins (1749-1836). In 1770 he proceeded to Bengal as a writer in the service of the East India Company. His interest in Sanskrit seems to have developed around 1778 when he helped establish a printing press for "Oriental" languages. His translation of the *Bhagavad-Gita* was issued in London in 1785 by the East India Company, Warren Hastings, the Governor General, writing an introduction extolling Wilkins' scholarship. There was no helpful exposition in this book of the Vedantic philosophy of the *Gita*. Nevertheless, this was the first translation of the *Bhagavad-Gita* into English,[34] two years before it was translated into French by J. P. Parraud. This translation into English soon brought Wilkins world-wide recognition as a Sanskrit scholar. In 1786 he left India for Bath for reasons of health but devoted part of his time to translating Sanskrit works. One of those is his translation of *Hitopadeśa*, as *Heetopades* of *Veeshnoo-Sarma*, which was published in Bath in 1787. Later, his *Radicals of Sanskrita Language* was published by the East India Company in London in the year 1808. All three of these important works were known and read in America. A discussion of these works by American readers is traced in the next chapter.

One of the most important British scholars of Sanskrit to be inspired by the ideals and achievement of the Asiatic Society

---

[33] *Biographie Universelle* (*Michaud*), Paris, n.d.
[34] London; C. Nourse.

of Bengal was Henry Thomas Colebrooke (1765-1837).[35]
Repelled by the gambling, drinking, and debauchery of the
Anglo-Indian community at Calcutta, Colebrooke turned to
administration.   He discovered that a precondition for efficient
legal administration of the country was a thorough knowledge
of the Hindu laws which could be known only through intensive
Sanskrit studies.   Sir William Jones had left the *Digest of Hindu
Laws* unfinished.   It was now being completed by a native
pundit, Jagannatha Tarkapanchanana.   The task called for a
scientifically trained scholar who was thoroughly familiar with
all the intricacies of interpreting Sanskrit codes of law and was
able to translate the same intricacies into English.   Colebrooke
was such a person.   In the midst of his several duties as judge
and revenue collector, he brought out his *Digest of Hindu Laws
on Contracts and Successions* in four volumes at Calcutta in
the year 1798.   He was appointed in 1805 to the chair of
Hindu Law and Sanskrit in the recently opened College of
Fort William in Calcutta.   Too busy to give lectures at the
College, he honored his appointment by undertaking *A Grammar
of the Sanskrit Language* which was published the same year in
Calcutta.   This was a methodical arrangement of the intricate
rules of Panini and his commentators and presented the merit
of the native grammarians in their true light.   In a small way
his work also foreshadowed the yet unborn science of comparative
philology.   During 1808 he published his famous essay, "On the
Vedas", in the *Asiatick Researches*.[36]   Until the appearance of
this essay, some European scholars had doubted the enthusiastic
claims of Sir William Jones.   But now most of those suspicions
were dispelled.   In a moderate and scholarly tone, Colebrooke
traced the history of how the sacred works of the Hindus had
been preserved and gave a descriptive account of the parts
and contents of the four *Vedas* and some *Upaniṣads*.   He testified
that the *Vedas* are genuine and that they have been regarded
as scripture for thousands of years.   For the first time, he
pointed out that "The whole of Indian theology is professedly
founded on the *Upaniṣads*".[37]   And what is the theology of the
Upaniṣads but Vedanta?   This essay remains an example of

[35] *DNB,* as in the cases which follow.
[36] VIII (London, 1808), pp. 377-497.
[37] *Ibid.,* p. 473.

precision, and absolute accuracy. Soon after its publication he was elected the President of the Asiatic Society of Bengal. Returning to England in 1814, he founded the Royal Asiatic Society of Great Britain and Ireland in the year 1823. He declined to be its first president but contributed a series of five major articles "On the Philosophy of the Hindus".[38] After his death in 1837, his English translation of *Sānkhyakārika* was published by Horace Hayman Wilson with the aid of the Oriental Translation Fund in London. His fourth essay "On the Philosophy of the Hindus" is subtitled "Vedanta", an essay providing a thorough exposition of the two systems of Vedanta. He quotes extensively from Bādarāyana's *Vedānta Sūtra* and explicates the text with the help of several native commentaries in Sanskrit. Of particular interest is his own comment which he offers by way of conclusion to this essay: "The notion, that the versatile world is an illusion (*māya*), that all which passes to the apprehension of the waking individual is but a phantasy presented to his imagination, and every seeming thing is unreal and is visionary, does not appear to be the doctrine of the text of *Vedānta*".[39]

In many respects Colebrooke's essays read like a textbook on Hindu systems of philosophy. Most of his essays were printed in popular collections and made available to readers as early as 1837. Any one who read these essays received a thorough introduction to Vedic literature and Vedantic philosophy. These essays were available in America both in the form of original articles appearing in the *Transactions* of the Asiatic Society of Great Britain and Ireland, and also in the popular collection, *Essays on the Religion and Philosophy of the Hindus*.[40]

Another British scholar to be inspired by the life and achievement of Sir William Jones was Horace Hayman Wilson (1786-1860).[41] In 1804 he left England for India as a surgeon, but commenced Oriental studies during the six-month voyage from London to Calcutta. Once in India, he intensified his

---

[38] In *Transactions of the Royal Asiatic Society of Great Britain and Ireland,* Vols. I and II (1823-1827); reprinted as *Essays on the Religion and Philosophy of the Hindus* (London; new edition, Williams and Norgate, 1858), pp. 208-242, subsequent references are to this edition.

[39] *Ibid.,* p. 242.

[40] *Ibid.*   [41] *DNB.*

Sanskrit studies and by 1813 he published an annotated text of Kalidasa's *Meghaduta*.[42]   By 1819 he completed his first edition of a *Sanskrit-English Dictionary* which he greatly improved when he brought out his second edition in 1832.[43]   This publication brought him high reputation and the reward of an appointment to the chair of Sanskrit at Oxford in 1832.   He now found time to work on some of the 549 Sanskrit manuscripts which he collected at Benares.   The most important result of his labors is the English translation of *Vishnu Purana*.[44]   In the same year 1840 also appeared his famous *Lectures on the Religions and Philosophical Systems of the Hindus*.[45]   According to one writer he promoted "a real knowledge of the very numerous branches of Indian learning which he made his own".[46]   He was an accomplished actor and this interest led him to translate several Sanskrit dramas as well, which he published under the title of *Select Specimens of the Theatre of the Hindus*.[47]   The above-mentioned works of his were known in the United States.   His translation of *Vishnu Purana* perhaps had wielded the most direct influence on American literature in inspiring Emerson to write the most intriguing of all his poems, "Hamatreya".   This influence is further discussed in the next chapter.

Another group of scholars who were responsible for searching the Hindu scriptures and translating some of them into English were the missionaries of Serampore.   Foremost among them was William Carey (1761-1834),[48] who arrived in India as the first Baptist Missionary in 1794.   For political reasons his work in Calcutta was not encouraged by the British.   In 1799 he removed to Serampore, which was then a Danish colony.   He established a printing press and a school and almost immediately translated the Bible into Bengali and published it.   With collaborators, he managed to translate the Bible into twenty-five other Indian languages as well.   Besides, he wrote a few grammars

---

[42] *Select Specimens of the Theatre of the Hindus,* 3 vols. (Calcutta, 1827).

[43] Calcutta.

[44] (London, 1840); reprinted in *Essays and Lectures Chiefly on the Religion of the Hindus,* 2 vols. (London, 1862).

[45] London.   [46] *DNB.*   [47] 3 vols. (Calcutta, 1827).

[48] *DNB.*   Also see *Life and Times of Carey, Marshman, and Ward* by John C. Marshman.

mostly to enable missionaries to learn Indian languages.[49] His linguistic reputation gained for him the chair of Sanskrit, Bengali, and Marathi in 1801 at the newly founded College of Fort William.

An associate who joined Carey in 1799 at Serampore was Joshua Marshman (1768-1837).[50] His assistance to Carey in translating the Bible into twenty-six Indian languages was appreciated not only in India and in England but in America too: Brown University in the United States granted him a degree of Doctor of Divinity in the year 1811. His subsequent interests shifted his concentration to Chinese studies. But in 1818 he established the first newspaper ever printed in an Eastern language, the *Samachar Durpan,* and in the same year he started publishing his monthly, *Friend of India.* Two years later he brought out a new periodical *The Quarterly Friend of India.* It was in these organs of opinion that Marshman entered into theological controversies with Raja Rammohan Roy, a controversy which, as we shall see, was to engage the attention of European and American theologians.

In this controversy, Marshman had a voluble supporter in another fellow missionary, William Ward (1769-1823).[51] Ward was a printer by profession but came under the influence of Carey whom he joined at Serampore in 1799 and helped print the Bible in twenty-six Indian languages. At the same time he cultivated proficiency in some of those Indian languages besides Sanskrit and translated some important Sanskrit works into English which he published in four volumes in 1811 under the title *Account of the Writings, Religion, and Manners of the Hindoos.*[52] This work is a conglomeration of extracts from the *Vedas, Puranas, Sastras,* and several commentaries. One of the pieces is a translation of a commentary called *Vedanta Sara,* which contains a brief summary of Vedanta philosophy. Ward's own comment on it is as follows:

The translation of the substance of the Vedanta Sara, ... may

---

[49] *Grammar of the Bengalee Language* (Serampore, 1801); *A Grammar of the Maharatta Language* (Serampore, 1805); *Grammar of the Sungskrit Language* (Serampore, 1806); *A Grammar of Punjabee Language* (Serampore, 1812); *A Grammar of the Telinga Language* (Serampore, 1814).
[50] *DNB.*   [51] *DNB.*   [52] Calcutta.

afford a specimen of the contents of the Darsansas — The
great similarity betwixt the Grecian and the Hindu schools of
the Philosophy, in their doctrines, prevailing disputes, &c.
has led him [H. T. Colebrooke] to form a conjecture respecting
the antiquity of the most celebrated of the Hindu sastras: and
he cannot help thinking that the Greek and Hindu literature
was at its zenith nearly at the same period; which idea seems
to be confirmed by the hints so often found in history, that
several of the Grecian philosophers visited the Hindu schools.[53]

Then he quotes the whole of Colebrooke's essay "On the Vedas"
because, according to Ward, it is the best essay on the subject.[54]
Some of Ward's remarks at the end of the essay should be of
special interest to the student of American literature: "Dr. Stiles,
president of Yale College in North America, formed such an
enthusiastic expectation from the amazing antiquity of the Hindoo
writings, that he actually wrote to Sir William Jones to request
him to search among the Hindoos for the Adamic books".[55]
Dr. Ezra Stiles was not a Sanskrit Scholar but he was proficient
in Arabic, Syriac, and Armenian, and one of his main interests
was Biblical history. Here is an instance of how a person who
is deeply immersed in Biblical history was led to search the
ancient Sanskrit writings in order to find probable collateral
evidence on the Biblical theory of creation. Instead, he found
Vedanta theory of Emanations. This is the way in which Biblical
scholars became familiar with Vedic literature and Vedantic
philosophy even when they were not intrinsically interested
in the Sanskrit language. Ward was subsequently entrusted
with the task of touring Europe and America to raise money for
the missionary College at Serampore, which brought him to
America late in 1820. In April 1821, he returned to India
via England. Ward's visit to America further heightened
American interest in India in general. In particular, his *Account
of the Writings* . . . came to be read by many churchmen and
seminarians who were seeking some kind of information on
India's religious and cultural heritage. Extracts from his
Account were published in London in 1822 under the title of

[53] *Ibid.*, I. p. vi.   [54] See pp. 72-73 of this book.
[55] William Ward, *Account of the Writings, Religion, and Manners of
the Hindoos* (Calcutta, 1811), vol. I, p. 302. I have not been able to
locate this letter.

A View of the History, Literature, and Mythology of the Hindoos . . . .[56] In this abridged form the American reader encountered another comprehensive account of the six systems of Hindu philosophy, two of which are Vedanta.[57]

Raja Rammohan Roy (1772-1833) was the most prominent personality who was an outstanding advocate of Vedanta philosophy and who challenged India to revive and popularize this philosophy first at home and then abroad. The Serampore missionaries were at first friendly but later entered into theological controversies with him and branded him as a heretic. Born into an affluent Bengali-Brahmin family, he received traditional education and early became proficient in Sanskrit, Persian, and Arabic. His open mind soon led him into a thorough investigation of the monotheistic religious thought of Islam, Judaism, and Christianity.

His studies directed him particularly to the universal theology of Vedanta and he soon undertook the translation of several Vedantic texts into Bengali and English. His *Abridgement of the Vedanta* was published in Calcutta in 1816 simultaneously in English, Bengali, and Hindustani. The same year also saw the publication of his English translations of *Kēna, Isa, Mandūka,* and *Kathā Upanisads* in separate volumes at Calcutta. The following year he published in Calcutta, his two volume work *A Defence of Hindu Theism.*[58]

As a result of his acquaintance with the missionaries at Serampore, he published in 1820 at Calcutta *The Precepts of Jesus,* subtitled, "the guide to Peace and Happiness; extracted from the Books of the New Testament ascribed to the four Evangelists, with translations in Sanskrit and Bengali". This book was printed by the Baptist Mission Press. Perhaps the missionaries felt that the precepts of Jesus cannot guarantee "Peace and Happiness" or that the doctrine of Grace was endangered. Whatever the reason the missionaries attacked Roy in reviews of this work. Roy countered their arguments with devastating irony in *An Appeal to the Christian Public in Defence*

[56] Published by Kingsbury, Parbury and Allen.

[57] Also see *Two Brahmin Sources of Emerson and Thoreau*, ed., by William B. Stein (Gainsville, Fla., 1967), pp. xvii and 113-292.

[58] *Rammohun Roy* by Iqbal Singh, 2 vols. (Bombay, 1958), hereafter cited as Iqbal Singh, *Rammohun Roy*.

of the Precepts of Jesus.[59]   About this time, he also collaborated
with Rev. William Adam and Rev. William Yates in translating
the four Gospels into Bengali from the original Greek. During
the translation, a semantic controversy rose over the Greek word
"dia" in the third verse of the first chapter of St. John's gospel.
It could have been translated either as "through" or "by" which
makes the verse read: "All things were made by Him". But
Roy, Adam and Yates felt that fidelity to the original indicated
the alternate rendering— "All things were made through Him".[60]
In the context of Roy's Vedantic beliefs, the latter rendering
almost amounted to asserting the Vedantic theory of creation by
emanation and contradicted the Church doctrine of creation by
God's command.   The subsequent theological controversies
separated Roy from the Trinitarian missionaries.   The irony of
the situation was that Rev. William Adam, the Baptist Missionary
who tried his best to convert Roy to Christianity, now turned
away from the Trinitarian doctrine.   Thus, in September 1821
at Roy's initiative, "the fallen second Adam" established a
Unitarian church in Calcutta. Most of its members were Scotsmen
in the service of the British India Company, but some were
followers of Roy.

The Unitarian nucleus soon brought Roy into limelight in
America where controversies over the divinity of Christ, the
virgin birth, and the resurrection were beginning to split the
Congregational Church and the breakaway free-thinkers were
only too glad to find a universal mind like Roy.   In the following
chapter we shall see how popular Roy was in America.   What
is important for us to note here are his translations of Vedic
literature and, through them, the availability of Vedantic philosophy to American readers.

Prior to 1840 some of these translations found another
channel through which to reach the common reader in the travel
descriptions of Lady Maria Callcott (1785-1842), who lived
and traveled for a few years in India.[61] Her *Journal of Residence
in India,* published in 1812 in London, became so popular that
another edition was brought out a year later.   Encouraged by
this success, she published her *Letters on India,* with etchings
and a map, in 1814.   This book soon became known in America.

[59] (Calcutta, 1820).   [60] Iqbal Singh, *Rammohun Roy,* I, 225.
[61] *DNB.*

Because of her style and easy narrative, it became a much discussed book in many homes in America. Using the epistolary method, she summarized almost all the researches of Sir William Jones, Charles Wilkins, H. T. Colebrooke, William Carey, Joshua Marshman, and William Ward. Moreover, Letters II to V are devoted entirely to Vedic literature and Vedantic philosophy.

Incidentally, Lady Callcott must have been aware of what the Americans were reading in the first two decades of the nineteenth century. Impressed by the theme of ventriloquism in the story of Chandraketu, who goes in search of Princess Vasavadatta, she compares it to the same theme in Charles Brockden Brown's *Wieland*.[62] Thus, even those Americans who were not directly interested in Sanskrit scholarship still encountered Vedic literature and Vedantic philosophy in a digested form, sometimes, in travelogues.

If American readers missed all the preceding works, they could have still been exposed to the riches of Vedic literature and Vedantic philosophy in the three volume *Historical and Descriptive Account of British India* by Hugh Murray, *et al.,* published in the Harper's Family Library series at New York in 1832. The first eight chapters of the first volume deal entirely with Vedic literature and Vedantic philosophy to the extent known at that time. The reasons suggested by the authors are as follows: "The theology, history, poetry, literature, and social condition of this remarkable people [Hindus] are all so closely interwoven, as to make it impossible satisfactorily to consider any one, unless in connection with all the rest".[63]

For nearly the same reasons, we had to consider in this chapter the work of the British and French adventurers, the British and French missionaries, most of them competent scholars but always with an ulterior motive, who approached Vedic literature and Vedantic philosophy. Their work caused histories, including those of philosophy, to be rewritten. Some of them made attempts at comparing their philosophies and literature with Vedantic philosophy and Vedic literature. Some of these comparisons became the fashion of the day. Some scholars inspired yet other scholars. All of them together lit a candle where earlier the dark night of ignorance prevailed.

[62] *Letters on India* (London, 1814), pp. 45-46; Charles Brockden Brown, *Wieland* (New York, 1796).   [63] P. 209.

5

EARLY AMERICAN DISCUSSION OF VEDIC LITERATURE AND VEDANTIC PHILOSOPHY

IN THE preceding chapters we have seen the efforts of remarkable scholar adventurers like Jones from England, Duperron from France, and Roy from India, who through their many persistent labors have translated several important selections from Vedic literature which contained, among other things, Vedantic ideas. We have also seen how the missionary impulse began to grow and create a new interest in the languages, literatures, culture, and religions of India. The same missionary impulse also gave a wider currency to much of the new found Vedic literature.

Doubtless, much of this literature was discussed in the drawing rooms of elite social and literary figures. But we have no record of their distinguished opinions even in the few diaries of the people who lived around the turn of the eighteenth century. The reason is that the later decades of the eighteenth century in America were years mainly devoted to political pamphleteering.

There is, however, a considerable body of concrete evidence in scholarly reviews and quarterlies indicating a small measure of interest in Vedic literature and Vedantic philosophy. It is now our task to sift this evidence and to assess the quality of this early American interest in Vedic literature and Vedantic philosophy.

It must be kept in mind that, unlike Britain and France, America did not have any colonial ties with India. Its interest was almost entirely humanitarian or evangelistic. Some of the early news reports about India in *The Boston Magazine* show primarily a compassionate concern about famine, epidemic, superstition, and war in India.[1] But with the availability of the Vedic translations of Sir William Jones and his successors, know-

[1] (Oct. 1783); (Nov. 1783); (March 1784).

ledge of the antiquity and profundity of Vedic literature and Vedantic philosophy also began to spread. In the early American reviews of Jones's life and his works one sees a detached scholarly interest.

The earliest American magazines that were published between 1741 and 1794 did not contain much original literary criticism. They paid even less attention to comparative literature. Frank Luther Mott euphemistically describes the magazines of this time as "eclectic" and remarks:

Probably at least three-fourths of the total contents of these magazines were extracted from books, pamphlets, newspapers, and other magazines, both English and American. Much the larger part of the selections was, of course, English. English books of travel, biography, and science gave up their choicest parts to the scissors of the magazine compiler.[2]

But this remark cannot be applied to the magazines that were published after the turn of the century. One can see a new fashion of erudite writing that displays a broad range of reading. Part of this new fashion relates to the opinions of Sir William Jones.

An example of this fashionable reference can be seen in the *Monthly Register: Magazine and Review of the United States* published in Charleston, South Carolina, and later during 1805 and 1807 in New York. The context is a review of *An Inquiry into the Present State of the Foreign Relations of the Union, as Affected by the Late Measure of Administration* published by Bradford of Philadelphia in 1806. The reviewer opens the discussion invoking the opinion of Sir William Jones in the following words:

It was the opinion of the *all accomplished* Sir William Jones that, in times of national adversity, those citizens are entitled to the highest praise, who by personal exertions, and active valour promote, at their private hazard the public welfare; that the second rank in the scale of honour is due to those, who in the great council of the nation, or, in other assemblies

[2] *A History of American Magazines* 1741-1850 (Cambridge, Mass., 1939), I, 39; hereafter cited as Mott.

legally concerned, propose and enforce, with manly eloquence, what they conceive to be salutary, or expedient on the occasion; and that the third place remains for those persons, who when they have neither a necessity to act, nor a fair opportunity to speak, impart in writing to their countrymen such opinions, as their reason approves, and such knowledge as their *painful researches* [italics mine] have enabled them to acquire.[3]

This review is signed "Independent American", very probably the pseudonym of Stephen C. Carpenter, the editor of the *Monthly Register*. Mott tells us that "Carpenter was an Englishman, who, after long service in India, had gained some journalistic fame by brilliant work in reporting the parliamentary speeches at the trial of Warren Hastings".[4] It is also probable that the "painful researches" quoted above is a reference to the then popular *Asiatick Researches* of the Asiatic Society of Bengal and of the Royal Asiatic Society of England.[5] The point to be noted here is that by 1807 oblique references to Sir William Jones and his writings in *Asiatick Researches* were meant to be recognized by the readers of scholarly reviews and magazines.

The immediate impact on American men of letters of Jones's English translations of Vedic literature can be seen in a series of "letter-essays" with the title "Letters of Shahcoolen, a Hindu Philosopher Residing in Philadelphia; to his Friend Al Hassan, an Inhabitant of Delhi", in the New York *Commercial Advertiser* as early as October 5, 1801. They were undersigned "Shahcoolen". A year later they were collected and published in book form by Russel and Cutler of Boston.[6] Cataloguers and historians first attributed these "Letters" to the pen of Samuel Lorenzo Knapp (1783-1838) who was a freshman at Dartmouth when the letters began to appear in the press. Ben Harris McClary maintains that they were authored by Benjamin Silliman (1779-1864).[7] Indeed Silliman's biographer writes,

---

[3] *Monthly Register, Magazine and Review of the United States* (Jan. 1807), p. 102.

[4] Mott, I, p. 260.

[5] See Chapter 3, p. 53 of this book.

[6] *Letters of Shahcoolen* (1802), introduction by Ben Harris McClary (Gainsville, Fla. 1962), hereafter cited as *Letters of Shahcoolen*.

[7] *Ibid.*, p. xvii.

"Mr. Silliman was early in life an occasional contributor to the news papers. A few years after graduation he wrote for the New York *Commercial Advertiser* which had been established by Noah Webster — a series of essays, some of them touching satirically on the follies of fashionable society. The idea appears to have been suggested by Goldsmith's 'Letters of a Chinese Philosopher'."[8] This is sufficient proof of Silliman's authorship of the "Letters", for they do contain satirical jibes at fashionable society. What is of special interest to us is that Silliman devotes four of these letters to a comparison of metaphor and image in *Gitagovinda* and *Song of Solomon*. Silliman may have come across the first English translation of Jayadeva's *Gitagovinda* done by Sir William Jones and published first in the *Asiatick Researches* as early as 1792 and again in *The Works of Sir William Jones* in 1799.[9] The translation itself in its original context is a continuation of a comparative study "On the Mystical Poetry of the Persians and the Hindus". By way of introduction, Jones wrote, "The loves of *CRISHNA* and *RADHA,* or, the reciprocal attraction between the divine goodness and the human soul, are told in the tenth book of *Bhagavat,* and are the subject of a little *Pastoral Drama,* entitled *Gitagovinda*". Jones's bowdlerization has already been mentioned. It is possible that Silliman was attracted to this particular poem out of a sense of mystic affinity with the portrayal of "the reciprocal attraction between the divine goodness and the human soul". He borrowed heavily from Jones's "Preface". Incidentally, this comparative study of image and verse may be described as the first American example of "intrinsic" criticism of comparative literature. Besides this study, Silliman also reported the nature of Hindu poetry by generously quoting from Jones's hymns to various Hindu deities. The most important of them is the "Hymn to Narayena".[10] It is important because in this hymn Jones discusses the Vedantic concepts of *māya* and *Brahman*. Though Silliman quotes the hymn in its entirety, he shows no evidence of understanding these concepts. He limits his comments only to a discussion of the

---

[8] George P. Fisher, *Life of Benjamin Franklin Silliman* (New York, 1866), pp. 55-56.

[9] III (London, 1792), pp. 165-207; and *Works* I (London, 1799), pp. 463-484.

[10] *Letters of Shahcoolen,* pp. 95-97.

imagery. Therefore, in *The Letters of Shahcoolen* we find an example of early American interest in Vedic literature, but not in Vedantic philosophy.

Towards the end of 1801 it becomes clear that libraries and learned societies considered it a matter of pride to acquire the available volumes of *The Works of Sir William Jones,* the *Asiatick Researches,* and the *Asiatick Miscellany* which contained many of Jones's hymns to Hindu deities. These, then, comprise a definite source of Vedic literature and Vedantic philosophy available in America. On Dec. 4, 1801, Samuel F. Bradford of Philadelphia made a present of *"Asiatic Researches*: and Asiatic Poems of Sir William Jones" to the American Philosophical Society. On this occasion he provided a written endorsement which is still in the Archives of the Society. A total of nine different works by Jones have reached about sixty libraries over the United States. At least nine of these libraries hold accession records that prove their acquisition of Jones's works by 1829.[11]

Part of the American demand for Jones's writings was met by the thirty-fifth volume of *The Works of the British Poets, with the Lives of the Authors,* edited by Robert Walsh Jr., and published by Samuel F. Bradford of Philadelphia in the year 1822. In this volume two hundred and forty-two pages out of a total of three hundred and ninety-six were devoted to Jones's poems and his life. Those selections were grouped under subheadings "Miscellanies", "Odes", "Tales", "Songs", and "Ballads". The life-sketch contains the usual American admiration of Jones's liberal views. His "Ode in Imitation of Alcaeus" which expressed his sympathies for American Revolution was, of course, included. "The Hymns", also, are presented in their entirety. Walsh took care to include Jones's "Argument" for each hymn. In the "Arguments" Jones commented upon the philosophical implication of the mythical deities. Thus, any reader of these hymns not only received a picture of the richness of Vedic imagery but also some information about the different concepts of Vedantic philosophy. "Camdeo", for example, was depicted not only as the Hindu Cupid but also as the "son of Maya, or the general attracting power".[12] A careful reader would have questioned the translation of *Māya* as "the general attracting

[11] See Chapter 3, p. 57 of this book.
[12] P. 123.

power", and would have suspected the inaccuracy of translating it merely as "illusions". Walsh makes no comment on the Vedantic ideas contained in these selections. It is very clear to us that Silliman certainly missed these ideas. And all this in spite of Jones making these Vedantic implication clear in the "Argument" of the "Hymn to Narayena" in the following words: "A complete introduction of the following Ode would be no less than a comment on the VADAS [Vedas] and the PURANS [Puranas] of the HINDUS, the remains of Egyptian and Persian Theology, and the tenets of Ionic and Italic schools; but this is not the place for so vast a disquisition".[13] Jones goes on to explain the Vedantic ideas he incorporated into each of his stanzas. "The third and the fourth stanza", he writes, "are taken from the Institutes of Menu [Manu] and the eighteenth Puran [Purana] of Vyasa.... From BREHME [defined] as *Brahman* in the first chapter of this book or the Great Being, in the neuter gender, is formed BREHMA [Brahma, the mythological person] in the masculine; and the second word is appropriated to the *creative power* of the Divinity".[14] As any modern reader can see, Jones in these words had offered one of the subtlest distinctions between a philosophical concept and a mythological deity. However, the facts only prove that these distinctions were lost on early American readers.

Next in importance is the eclecticism of the Phi Beta Kappa Society whose members showed an active interest in reading *Asiatick Researches*. In 1806, they had a serial feature entitled "Primitive History", in their magazine *Literary Miscellany* published in Boston. In the first feature article in 1805 there are three footnote references to *Asiatick Researches*. They have also included Jones's "Ode in Imitation of Alcaeus",[15] which only proves the fashion of referring to Jones. None of their articles indicates any comprehension of Vedantic concepts or a discussion of them.

This interest in Jones and his researches, of course, did not evaporate suddenly. It persisted for quite some time. Nearly twenty years after the publication of the *Literary Miscellany*, Professor Edward Everett (1794-1865) "pronounced" an

---

[13] *Ibid.,* p. 174.
[14] *Ibid.,* p. 175.
[15] *Literary Miscellany,* I (1805), p. 301.

"Oration" before the Phi Beta Kappa Society at Cambridge on August 27, 1824. In his usually grand rhetoric he reminded his listeners:

> How much have we heard, too, of the mutual advancement of the Hindoos, their numerous writings in theology, metaphysics, astronomy, grammar, music, their logicians, mathematicians, and poets. Sir William Jones, the best judge of this subject, that ever lived, speaks with rapture of some of these works, and says, that, in addition to many beautiful specimens of lighter poetry among the Hindoos, their epic is 'magnificent and sublime in the highest degree'. The Sanscrit language is represented as susceptible of polished, elegant, and expensive style of composition, to which hardly any other language can aspire. And, moreover, is it not true, that the East was the fountain of knowledge of the West? The very laws, that gave a semblance of stability to the Athenian democracies, were gleaned from Egypt, and to Egypt they came from Chaldea and India. The laws of Solon and the philosophy of Plato, were little else than transcripts of what they had borrowed from the wise men of other countries.[16]

This opinion of Edward Everett once again proves the fashion of referring to Jones and his researches. It must also be noted that Professor Everett's description of the East as "the fountain of knowledge to the West" borders on the romantic in terms of the value attributed to the East.

Quite apart from these fashionable references to Jones's discoveries and researches, the learned journals also evidence a growing missionary interest in the religions and social customs of India. The *North American Review* of June, 1819, published an article entitled "Manners and Customs of India".[17] This is a lengthy review of *A Description of the Manners and Customs of the Hindoos* by the Abbé J. A. Dubois.[18] The reviewer may have been Edward T. Channing, who edited the *North American Review* at this time. He was known for an "unornate style"

[16] *NAR*, XX (April 1825), p. 433, quoted in a review of "Professor Everett's Orations".

[17] IX, pp. 36-58.

[18] See Chapter 4, p. 67 of this book.

and this article meets that description. In this article one finds reference to Vedantic ideas reported by Dubois. For instance, the reviewer notes: "The unity and the infinite perfection of the Deity is announced in their Vedas — not ambiguously or by implication but openly and directly and without reserve...."[19] He also understands that "Many of their [the Hindu] Pundits are Theists in the strictest sense of the word".[20] To prove his point he quotes the exact words of Dubois:

> "God" to use the words of the philosophers of India, "is an immortal Being, pure and unmixed, without qualities, form or division; the Lord and Master of all things. He extends over all, sees all, directs all, without beginning and without end". Power, strength and gladness dwell with Him. This is but a slight sketch of the lofty terms in which the Hindu writings, after their philosophers, describe the *Para-Brahma,* or Supreme Being.[21]

This quotation proves that the reviewer was impressed by the summary of Hindu philosophy, which is of the Vedantic school. This does not mean that the reviewer knew this as Vedantic philosophy. In fact his quotation does not end here. It continues:

> 'There philosophers soon separated into two parties, upon the nature of God and that of the Universe. Up to the present times, each has its numerous partizans. The first is called Dwitam [*dvaita* school of Vedanta], the sect of two; that is to say, those who hold the existence of two beings or substances, namely, God and the world which He created, and to which He is united. The other sect is called Adwitam [*advaita* school of Vedanta], not two; meaning those who acknowledge but one Being, one substance, one God'.[22]

The two schools mentioned in this paragraph are the two schools of Vedantic philosophy. This, in fact, is a very specialized kind of reportage of Vedanta. The quotation from Dubois' description does not stop here either. It goes on and covers still another important concept of Vedantic philosophy, *māya.*

[19] *NAR,* IX (June 1819), p. 38.   [20] *Ibid.,* p. 39.
[21] *Loc. cit.*   [22] *Ibid.,* pp. 39-40.

'These professors of the last doctrine, designate the foundation of the system, by the two technical expressions *Abhavana Bhava-Nasti* [italics mine], from nothing, nothing comes. They maintain that creation is an impossibility, and that on the other hand, a pre-existing and eternal substance is absolutely chimerical. From these premises they infer that whatever we imagine to be the universe and the various objects which appear to compose it, is nothing but a pure illusion or Maya'.[23]

The reviewer however does not seem to agree with this definition of *māya*. So in a tone that is confident of the accuracy of his knowledge he offers the following contradictory opinion: "Our author does not seem to be aware that while the Hindu ideologists deny the existence of matter, they admit that the unceasing operation of divine energy causes the appearances, the aggregate of which we term the universe".[24]

The reviewer's definition of *māya* is certainly closer to the one enunciated in the first chapter of this dissertation. In the rest of the article the reviewer does not appear to be promoting Vedantic philosophy. He deviates into a discussion of the polytheistic nature of "popular Hinduism". It is consoling to a student of Vedanta that at least one early American writer saw this distinction between intellectual Vedanta and "popular Hinduism".

In America, prior to 1840, references to Vedic literature also appear in the form of articles reviewing Classical Sanskrit plays. In 1826 Horace Hayman Wilson published in Calcutta his translation of two ancient Sanskrit plays under the title, *Select Specimens of the Theatre of the Hindus*. Within two years this work must have reached America, for in January 1828, it was reviewed in the *North American Review*.[25] The review supplies us with no special information on the early American interest in Vedic literature other than the reviewer's ability to summarize at least one of the two plays in Wilson's anthology. There are, of course, the customary references to the *Works* of Sir William Jones and to the *Asiatick Researches*.[26] Incidentally, the reviewer tells us in a footnote that Kalidasa's play in Jones's English translation was so popular in America that it was republished in

---

[23] *Loc. cit.*   [24] *Loc. cit.*

[25] XXVI, pp. 111-126.   [26] *Ibid.*, pp. 112 and 125 respectively.

Boston in *The Emerald,* a weekly devoted largely to a discussion of drama.[27] "Sacontala" and the two plays translated by Wilson are Vedic literature by our definition, though they contain no explicit Vedantic concepts. The review under discussion, then, is another instance of early American interest in Vedic literature, but not in Vedantic philosophy.

One sure opportunity for direct contact with Vedantic philosophy, however, did present itself as early as March 1818 in the form of an article in the *North American Review.* Its title "The Theology of the Hindoos, as Taught by Ram Mohun Roy",[28] suggests how close the writer, William Tudor, came to an understanding of Vedanta. Quoting from three important works of Roy, Tudor explains. "The scriptures, or the sacred books of the Hindoos, are called the Vedas. . . . These books contain the doctrines of the Hindoo religion".[29] The tone and the approach in these perliminary statements seem intended to educate the American readers. "We have dwelt the longer on this subject", continues Tudor, "because it is likely hereafter to attract much attention".[30] Then he presents several excerpts from Roy's writings, mainly from *Translation of an Abridgment of the Vedant,*[31] or *Resolution of all the Veds,* and *Translation of Ishopanishad.*[32]

In the concluding paragraph of this article, Tudor observes:

Ram Mohun is not a Christian, it is true, but the doctrine he inculcates differs very little from the Christian doctrine respecting the nature and attributes of the Deity. It is the same in its spirit and objects.

The tone and the reasoning of this observation is Universalist Unitarian. In early America, it is a rare case of recognition of affinities between some forms of Christian thought and some

[27] Mott, I, 247.

[28] VI, pp. 386-393. [29] *Ibid.,* p. 386. [30] *Ibid.,* p. 393.

[31] Subtitled, *Likewise a Translation of the Cena Upanishad;* with a Preface by John Digby and a *Letter Addressed to Him by Rammohun Roy* (London, 1817).

[32] With a running subtitle, *One of the Chapters of the Yajoor Ved; According to the Commentary of the celebrated Shankaracharya; Establishing the Unity and Incomprehensibility of the Supreme Being; and that his worship alone can lead to Eternal Beatitude* (Calcutta, 1816).

doctrines of Vedanta. Yet, Tudor had no way of explaining the doctrine of *māya* because Roy himself had underplayed its importance in his exposition of Vedantic "theology". Therefore, once again we are led to admit that Vedantic philosophy in its systematic form was not made available to early American readers.

Other reviewers of Roy's writings were far behind William Tudor in appreciating Vedantic ideas. For instance, the anonymous reviewer of the *Analytic Magazine* of Philadelphia[33] had a low opinion of Vedic literature and Vedantic philosophy in spite of referring to H. T. Colebrooke's famous essay "On the Vedas".[34] He writes:

> Rammohun Roy, teaching the unity of God on the principle of the Vedas, is indeed like a sculptor endeavoring to form a statue from a mass of coarse and crude materials, which are incapable of admitting elegance of form, or the display of excellence of workmanship.[35]

William Cullen Bryant, for instance, reviewed Roy's *Precepts of Jesus*[36] in *New York Review and Athenaeum Magazine*[37] of June 1825, without revealing any special understanding of the Vedantic philosophy of Roy.

Adrienne Moore supplies us with a thorough list of the American magazines which discussed Roy's life and writings.[38] She traces the interest of the Unitarian Missionary Movement in Roy and his thought. The Unitarian periodical, *Christian Register,* she points out, gave wide publicity to Roy's works and thought. She reports that Roy's name was mentioned 136 times in this magazine alone. One of his letters written from Calcutta on January 13, 1824, addressed to David Reed, was printed in *Christian Register,* May 7, 1824.[39] But an appreciation of Roy, such as the writings in *Christian Register* maintained, hardly attests to an appreciation of Vedantic philosophy. The Unitarian

[33] XV (Feb. 1820), pp. 129-147.
[34] *Asiatic Researches,* VIII, London, 1808, pp. 377-497. Also see Chapter 4, p. 72 of this book.
[35] *Op. cit.,* p. 147.
[36] *The Guide to Peace and Happiness...* (Calcutta, 1820).
[37] I (June 1825), pp. 447-453.
[38] *Rammohun Roy and America* (Calcutta, 1942).
[39] III, p. 154.

interest in Roy is in order to gain a prominent Hindu convert. We know that there was correspondence between Roy and Dr. Joseph Tuckerman, the head of the Unitarian Missionary Movement. Similar correspondence also took place between Roy and Rev. Henry Ware.[40] Ware, for example, wrote to Roy inquiring about the desirability of evangelizing India. Roy's reply was published in Calcutta as *A Letter to the Reverend Henry Ware on the Prospects of Christianity in India,*[41] in which Roy made it very clear that the prospects were rather slim.

The American Baptist Magazine, published since September 1803 by the Baptist Missionary Society of Massachusetts, carried extensive reports on the progress of the missionary work in India. But not one of those articles shows any willingness to see Vedic literature and Vedantic philosophy as worth recognition or approval.

James Marsh (1794-1842), Professor of Oriental Languages at the Hampden-Sidney Theological School in Virginia from 1824 to 1825 did not plunge into Vedic studies. His proficiency in "Oriental" languages, in the manner of Dr. Ezra Stiles, is limited only to Middle-Eastern languages. His interest in transcendental philosophy is based mainly upon the mysticism of S. T. Coleridge, whose *Aids to Reflection* he edited in 1829 when he was President of the University of Vermont and taught "moral and intellectual philosophy". He may have come across Degerando's book *Histoire Compareè de Systémes de Philosophie* and his *Du Perfectionnement Moral.*[42] But he does not seem to have cultivated a special interest in Vedic literature, nor does he seem to derive any of his transcendental ideas from Vedantic philosophy. He remained a "Christian" transcendentalist.

The reviewers seem to be totally unaware of Duperron's *Oupnek'hat*. Not a single review of this work can be found in any of the early American magazines. Neither do the reviewers pay any attention to the content of the histories of philosophy[43] that began to pay attention to Vedic literature and Vedantic philosophy.

Therefore, we are led to the conclusion that the early American interest in Vedic literature was of a passing nature. It was caused

[40] *Op. cit.,* pp. 149-150.
[41] 1829.   [42] See Chapter 4, p. 66 of this book.
[43] See Chapter 4, p. 65 of this book.

partly by the affection Americans had for Jones, partly by the fashion of quoting Jones and the *Asiatick Researches,* partly by evangelistic concern, and partly out of a romantic love of the remote and the exotic. This interest produced such comparative studies of poetry as in Silliman's "Letters of *Shahcoolen* (1802)". But even this was limited to a comparison of metaphor and verse. William Tudor, Edward Everett, and the anonymous reviewer of Dubois' *Description of the Manners and Customs of the Hindus* did appear to be impressed by the Vedantic ideas they stumbled upon. They show a romantic kind of appreciation of such ideas as "the Unity of the Infinite Being", but none of them seemed to have been aware of the system of philosophy known as Vedanta. They paid no attention to H. T. Colebrooke's masterful essay "On the Vedas"[44] in which he presented a scholarly summary of Vedantic philosophy. Their interest in Roy's teachings often turned into a gossipy review of popular Hindu polytheism. Their achievement is in building and maintaining a mild interest in Vedic literature and in informing their reading public of the existence of a rich body of literature and of highly developed systems of philosophy in India.

[44] *Asiatic Researches,* VIII (London, 1808), pp. 377-497.

6

CONCLUSION: EARLY VEDIC READINGS BY AMERICAN TRANSCENDENTALISTS

WE HAVE seen, in the preceding chapters, how modern scholarship defines Vedantic ideas and how those ideas determine a monistic worldview. We have seen how the English, German, and French scholars have taken the first steps in discovering Vedic literature and how those scholars have explicated those Vedantic ideas. Then, we have seen how the growing missionary interest in evangelizing India had resulted in more English translations of Vedic literature. We have seen the efforts of Rammohun Roy in presenting an apology for "Vedantic Monotheism". We have seen, too, the manner in which this literature and philosophy were made available in American libraries. We have seen also how some of the reviewers in American scholarly periodicals were impressed by certain Vedic passages containing profound Vedantic ideas. But they have often restricted themselves to a discussion of the polytheism of popular Hinduism.

We must, now, find out if the same material reached the chief American transcendentalists — Emerson, Thoreau, and Whitman. We must also find out if, in addition to reading the available Vedic literature, they accepted Vedantic philosophy over and above any other system of philosophy which was also available to them. If they did not accept it, then, were they at least receptive to Vedic literature and Vedantic philosophy? In pursuing this line of enquiry, we shall have to stop at July 1842, the year in which "ethnical scriptures" appeared in *The Dial*.[1] In an editorial note Emerson explains the purpose:

We commence in the present number the printing of a series

[1] "Veeshnoo Sarma", pp. 82-85; and "The Laws of Menu" (January 1843), pp. 331-340.

of selections from the oldest ethical and religious writings of men, exclusive of the Hebrew and Greek Scriptures.   Each nation has its bible more or less pure; none has yet been willing or able in a wise and devout spirit to collate its own with those of other nations, and sinking the civil-historical and the ritual portions to bring together the grand expressions of the moral sentiment in different ages and races, the rules for guidance of life, the bursts of piety and abandonment to the Invisible and the Eternal; — a work inevitable sooner or later, and which we hope is to be done by religion and not by literature.[2]

Emerson then presents us with four pages of excerpts from Charles Wilkins' translation of "Heetopades" of Vishnoo Sarma. He picks up this series again six months later and offers us this note: "In pursuance of the design animated in our Number of July, to give a series of *ethnical scriptures* [Italics mine], we subjoin our extracts from the Laws of Menu."[3]   These Vedic excerpts in the form of "ethnical scriptures" demonstrate American interest in Vedic literature and Vedantic philosophy, by July 1842.   But prior to this time what was the degree of American interest in Vedic literature ?

An examination of the *Journals and Miscellaneous Notebooks of Emerson*[4] proves that his early opinion of India was limited to the superstitious polytheism of popular Hinduism.   His early references to India do not acknowledge the existence of Vedic literature available to him.   He had not discovered Vedic literature or Vedantic philosophy prior to 1830.   In "Wide World I" Emerson made the following entry on April 10, 1820: "It was remarked in the *Quarterly Review* that as you go west superstition grows more fanatical and inhuman; i.e., Hindustan is more cruel in her ceremonies (?) and punishments (?) than Egypt, and Egypt than Europe."[5]   Emerson, of course, was carelessly paraphrasing Robert Southey's review of Thomas D. Fosbrooke's British Monachism (*sic*)," in the thirteenth

[2] (July, 1842), p. 82.

[3] (January 1843), p. 331.

[4] Ed. by William H. Gilman, *et al.*, 7 vol. (Cambridge, Mass., 1960). So far only seven volumes have been published.   They cover Emerson's Journals from 1819-1940.   This work is hereafter cited as E. *JMN*.

[5] *Ibid.*, I, pp. 14, 15, n. 22.

volume of the *Quarterly Review*.[6] He changed the sense of the opening sentence of Southey's article which actually is: "Superstition has always lost something of its grossness as it proceeded from East to West." During the same year, in another journal which he called "Notebook XVIII," Emerson wrote: "The ostentatious rituals of Egypt and India which worshipped God by outraging nature though softened as it proceeded west was still too harsh a discipline for Athenian manners to undergo."[7] This opinion too is clearly an echo of Southey's remarks mentioned above. In addition, Emerson must have begun reading Southey's "Curse of Kehama" during 1820. Some time before April 21, 1820, Emerson read a poem before the Pythologian Club of Harvard College. The title of the poem is "Improvement" and it contains references to the state of India in the manner described by Southey in his "curse" of 1810. Five lines in Emerson's poem illustrate the low opinion of India he had at this time:

> And bid Improvement rise on Indian plains
> That land of woe & of romantic strains
> There in devotion to mysterious powers
> The Indian stands in Ganges' holy bowers
> On the hot sands where human nature fails....[8]

A few days earlier on April 14, 1821, Emerson wrote the poem "Indian Superstition" to satisfy an academic requirement. This poem seems to have been placed in The Harvard College Exhibition of April 24, 1821.[9] As its title announces, it is about the superstitious rites of the Hindus. It bears a close resemblance to Southey's "Curse".

The following extracts from "Indian Superstition" illustrate the youthful Emerson's preoccupation with the exotic superstitions of popular Hinduism. He has not yet suspected the existence of Vedantic philosophy in India. The India of Emerson's youth is:

---

[6] (July 1819), p. 66.
[7] *Op. cit.*, I, p. 210.   [8] *Ibid.*, I, p. 240-241.
[9] Ed. by Kenneth W. Cameron (Hanover, N. H., 1954), p. 7; reprinted in *ESQ*, III Quarter (1963).

Far o'er the East where boundless Ocean smiles,
And greets the wanderer to his thousand isles,
Dishonoured India clanks her sullen chain,
And wails her desolation to the main.

To Emerson the gods of India had none of the fascination that they had for Jones who wrote beautiful "Hymns" for several of them. To Emerson these gods are "fiends," and "demons." For, in lines 25 and 26 of the above poem, he writes:

O'er men the car of fiends tremendous rolled,
On high the laugh of demons scared the bold.

"The car of fiends" no doubt is the "Juggernaut" and these ideas seem to have come from Southey. Unfortunately, Southey himself knew little about Vedic scriptures. Therefore, Emerson could derive no scholarly information from Southey. In line 55 he writes: "Bewildered fancies in his scriptures tell —." "Bewildered fancies," indeed, was the opinion he entertained at this point about Vedic literature. And this, in spite of exposure in 1820 to the riches of Vedic literature he must have come across in Sir John Shore, Lord Teignmouth's *Life of Sir William Jones,*[10] in which was given not only a description of how Jones discovered Vedic literature but also how Jones translated and used some of it to write his several "Hymns" to Hindu deities. This book was borrowed by Emerson from the Boston Library Society on December 21, 1820.[11] He makes no excerpts and makes no comments on the life or works of Sir William Jones. On the other hand his journals of this year contain several extracts from Southey.

Between 1820 and 1822 there is only one reference to "Menu" in his journals. But this quotation from "Menu" does not come from Jones's translation but from a footnote in Southey's "curse." Emerson himself acknowledges the source: "These Indian doctrines are quoted in Notes to Curse of Kehama."[12] His usage of the phrase "Indian doctrines" is misleading because his quotation in the journal is one of the *ordinances* of "Menu" and this particular passage has nothing to do with "Indian doctrines."

[10] (London, 1804).
[11] E. *JMN,* I, pp. 56-57, n.   [12] E. *JMN,* I, p. 340.

All this leads us to believe that Emerson had not yet discovered the idealism of Vedantic philosophy in spite of reading *Asiatick Miscellany* sometime between 1819 and 1824 according to his "Catalogue of Books Read."[13] His journals of these years give us no evidence of his borrowing any idea or transcribing any passage from this work which contained many of the "Hymns" of Jones.

One of these "Hymns" is a "Hymn to Narayena." It is in the "argument" to this hymn that Jones explained Vedantic ideas. Benjamin Silliman seems, as we have seen, to have appreciated at least the poetic beauty of this hymn.[14] But Emerson seems to have missed even that.

On July 6, 1822, however, he copied the last ten lines of the "Hymn to Narayena" in his journal. One might suppose, as Arthur Christy did, that Emerson copied it from one of the works of Sir William Jones.[15] This was not so. He got those lines from a letter written to him by his aunt, Mary Moody Emerson.[16] The entries in the journal preceding the transcript of "Hymn to Narayena" show that Emerson was groping for suitable passages to express his vague ideas about the universality of God. He concluded those ideas in the following manner: "I know of nothing more fit to conclude the remarks which have been made in the last pages than certain fine pagan strains."

Of dew-bespangled leaves and blossoms bright,
Hence ! vanish from my sight,
Delusive pictures ! unsubstantial shews !
My soul absorbed, one only Being knows,
Of all perceptions, one abundant source,
Hence every object, every moment flows,
Suns hence derive their force,
Hence planets learn their course;
But suns and fading worlds I view no more,
God only I percieve, God only I adore ![17]

---

13 *Ibid.,* I, p. 396.
14 Chapter 5, p. 83 of this book.
15 Christy, pp. 68-69.
16 *The Letters of Ralph Waldo Emerson,* ed. by Ralph L. Rusk in 6 Vols. (New York and London, 1966), I, p. 116, n. 22: hereafter cited as E. *L.*   17 E. *JMN,* I, pp. 153-154.

In describing them as "certain fine pagan strains" Emerson betrays his unawareness of Jones's authorship of these lines. Apparently many scholars including William H. Gilman who edited the *Journals and Miscellaneous Notebooks* of Emerson have believed that this "Hymn to Narayena" was a "translation of an Indian hymn."[18] They are wrong. This hymn was composed by Jones who captured the imagery and the philosophy of Vedic literature. That Emerson transcribed it in his journal indicates that he was impressed by the philosophical purport of the poem.

One would suppose that after encountering profound Vedantic ideas in the "Hymn to Narayena", Emerson would be inclined to look for more of them by diligently searching in Vedic literature, but a journal entry on January 19, 1823, shows that he was still preoccupied with the superficial absurdities of "Hindoo mythology". In his words, "The idolatry of every nation has had a tendency towards this belief that the arm of Omnipotence could be chained down by sacrifice and entreaty, which the Hindoo mythology has pursued to extravagant lengths."[19]

On December 12, 1823 he makes another entry touching upon Hindu mythology: "The Indian Pantheon is of prodigious size; 330 million Gods have in it each their heaven, or rather each their parlour, in this immense 'goddery.' 'In (its) quantity & absurdity their superstition has nothing to match it, that is or ever was in the world.' "[20] This note is a summary of two articles he read in *Edinburgh Review*. One of those articles is a review of William Ward's books, *Account of the Writings, Religion, and Manners of the Hindoos ...* and *A View of the History, Literature and Religion of the Hindoos....*[21] In spite of the fact that the reviewers of the above mentioned works touched upon Vedic literature and Vedantic philosophy, we find Emerson once again limiting himself to remarks on Hindu mythology. At any rate, he does not seem to have been inspired sufficiently at this point to dip into those English translations of Vedic literature supplied by Ward.

---

[18] *Ibid.*, I, p. 154, n. 69.

[19] *Ibid.*, II, p. 86.

[20] *Ibid*, II, p. 195.

[21] The articles Emerson read are from *The Edinburgh Review*, XXIX (Nov. 1817), pp. 141-164; (Feb. 1818), pp. 377-403 respectively.

Sometime between October and December 1830, Emerson began reading Degerando's work on comparative philosophies.[22] From Degerando's *Histoire Comparée des Systèmes* . . . . ,[23] he makes the following summary and translation: "Idealism a primitive theory. The Mahabharat one of the *sacred books of India* [italics mine] puts in the mouth of Tschak Palak these express words. 'The senses are nothing but the soul's instrument of action; no knowledge can come to the soul by their channel.' (*Vide* L'Oupnek-hat par Anquetil Duperron, t[ome]. I. p. 467)."[24] The reference to Anquetil Duperron is that of Degerando[25] which Emerson copied verbatim. Emerson's knowledge of Duperron's work *L'Oupnek'hat* then, was derived from a secondary source, Degerando's *Histoire Comparée des Systèmes,* and from a mere footnote. Nevertheless, scholars like Arthur Christy and those that relied on him were led to believe that Emerson had read Duperron's *L'Oupnek'hat.*[26] Emerson probably never saw Duperron's *L'Oupnek'hat,* much less read it.

The most important point to be noted here in this journal entry is that for the first time Emerson has come to believe that there are 'sacred books of India,' i.e., Vedic literature. For the first time we find Emerson referring to the spirituality of Vedic literature. It is probable that after Emerson read Degerando in December 1830, his attitude towards Vedic literature and Vedantic philosophy began to broaden. This view, that Emerson's interest in Vedic literature and Vedantic philosophy began to take seed after reading Degerando, contradicts his own assurance which he made in a letter to a Sanskrit scholar, Max Muller, in 1873. In that letter Emerson wrote: "I remember I owed my first taste for this fruit [Vedic Literature] to Cousin's sketch, in his first Lectures of the Dialogue between Krishna and Arjoon. . . ."[27] One might say

---

[22] See Chapter 4, p. 65 of this book.

[23] Vol. I, p. 254.

[24] E. *JMN,* III, p. 362.

[25] *Histoire Comparée des Systèmes de Philosophie,* I (Paris, 1822), p. 254, n. 1.

[26] Christy, p. 284; "Emerson and India", unpublished Ph.D. Dissertation by Man Mohan Singh, University of Pennsylvania, 1947, p. 27.

[27] E. *L,* I, p. lix.

that during 1830 Emerson's interest in Vedic literature was beginning to germinate. It was to grow, bloom, and yield fruit.

By May 1836 we find him quoting "Menu" from primary sources in English translation: "Put in the sermon to Scholars the brave maxim of the code of Menu; 'A teacher of the Veda should rather die with his learning than sow it in sterile soil, even though he be in grievous distress for subsistence.' "[28]   This quotation comes verbatim from *Institutes of Hindu Law: or, The Ordinances of Menu* . . . translated by Sir William Jones (London, 1825), p. 18.   Though this passage may be called Vedic literature, it does not contain any Vedantic ideas.   It displays, of course, one unique quality which is peculiar to Vedantists, i.e., Brahmanical supermanlike exclusivism.   It is surprising that Emerson should be impressed by such exclusivism. One might say that his interest at this point in Vedic literature and "Menu" smacks of the fashion of the times, i.e., quoting exotic sources in support of personal views.

Yet we find him giving expression to an idea that is uniquely Vedantic when on May 26, 1837, he wrote in his journal: "Who shall define to me an Individual ?   I behold with awe & delight many illustrations of the One Universal Mind.   I see my being imbedded in it.   I am only a form of him.   He is the soul of Me. I can even with a mountainous aspiring say, *I am God....* "[29] "I am God", *aham brahmasmi* is precisely one of the basic conclusions of Vedantic philosophy.   We have no evidence to prove that Emerson arrived at this conclusion with the help of his readings in Vedic literature.   This probably is the culmination of his monistic speculations, but it is only natural that after reaching such a conclusion, Emerson should take a deeper interest in Vedic literature and Vedantic philosophy.

Kenneth W. Cameron's account of Emerson's reading shows that he had not plunged into a serious study of Vedic literature until 1855.[30]   But Emerson's journals show that between July 23 and September 22, 1840, he borrowed volume III of the *Works of Sir William Jones* from which he excerpted several passages.   These passages consist of fifty-two ordinances of "Menu."   Emerson chose them from different chapters of the

[28] E. *JMN*, V, p. 165.

[29] *Ibid.*, V, p. 336.

[30] *Ralph Waldo Emerson's Reading* (Raleigh, N. C., 1941), p. 29.

Institutes of Hindu Law in the third volume of Jones's *Works*. This volume was withdrawn from Boston Athenaeum on July 23 and returned on September 22, 1840.[31] It is probable that it was Emerson who borrowed this volume at this time because it was during these dates that he made excerpts from "Menu" in his journal. The fact that he excerpted these passages proves only that he has just begun to seek deliberately to find whatever Vedic literature in whatever form was available to him in 1840. Hitherto, he came upon it by chance, once in a letter from his Aunt Mary Moody Emerson and several other times in book reviews in periodicals and most often from the footnotes of Southey's poem "The Curse of Kehama."

Except for ten passages, these fifty-two ordinances of "Menu" were not the same as the ones which appear in *The Dial* of January 1843.[32] The selections in *The Dial* are ascribed to Thoreau by George W. Cooke.[33] Unfortunately, in a copy of *The Dial* at the Michigan University Library somebody has scribbled in ink the misleading note, "Probably by Emerson". The selections in *The Dial* do not exactly match the passages Emerson has entered in his diary. Therefore, it is reasonable to think that George W. Cooke was correct in ascribing *The Dial* selections to Thoreau.

When we turn to Thoreau for his interest in Vedic literature prior to 1842, we are bound to be disappointed, for he did not keep a journal until he was advised to do so, probably by Emerson, in 1837. His first entry of October 22, 1837 reads: " 'What are you doing now?' he asked, 'Do you keep a journal?' So I make my first entry today."[34] There is no evidence in his journal of the following two years proving Thoreau's discovery of Vedic literature. Nevertheless, like Emerson, he must have come across Southey's "Curse." He must have also perused some articles on India in the *Quarterly Review* and *Edinburgh Review* which treated Hindu scriptures mostly as a curious product of wild, idolatrous, and depraved imagination. But

---

[31] E. *JMN*, VI, pp. 392-397.   [32] III, pp. 331-340.

[33] *An Historical and Biographical Introduction to Accompany THE DIAL*, II (New York, 1961), p. 206.

[34] *The Journal of Henry David Thoreau*, ed. by Bradford Torrey and Francis H. Allen, I (Cambridge, Mass., 1961), p. 4; hereafter cited as T. *J.*

unlike Emerson, he does not comment on the exotic aspects of popular Hinduism. Therefore, the absence of any comparably derogatory reference to Hindu superstitions in his journal entries should be noted and interpreted as evidence allowing for his reverent and receptive attitude to Vedic literature which he was to encounter in 1840. Thoreau at least did not have to clear his mind, as Emerson probably had to, of hastily preconceived opinions on superstitions in Hinduism. Therefore, we find, on August 28, 1840, Thoreau writing in his journal: "The fowls which are elsewhere domesticated run wild in India, and so I think of these domestic thoughts and fashions when I read the Laws of Menu."[35] Thoreau, here, is giving vent to his admiration of the freedom of speculation he encountered in the "Laws of Menu."

Perry Miller believes that Thoreau read Degerando's *Histoire Comparée des Systèmes. . . .* (Paris, 1804-22) during 1840-41 and that it was in this work that he first encountered "oriental philosophy."[36] But Thoreau did not stop there. He went ahead and read the available Vedic literature.

On May 31, 1841 in a journal entry Thoreau refers to "The Laws of Menu with the Gloss of Culluca."[37] On August 9, 1841 we find him referring again to "Menu."[38] On September 2, 1841 we find him still preoccupied with "Menu" and the "Vedas."[39] A few months later, on March 23, 1842, we find him referring to Sir William Jones and the Vedas.[40] The very next day we find him referring to "Veeshnoo Sarma," the author of "Heetopades" translated into English by Charles Wilkins in 1876.[41] The last two journal entries, referred to here, were later used by Thoreau in *A Week on the Concord and Merrimack Rivers.*[42] Though *A Week* was meant to describe the voyage he made during August 1839, the book itself was not published till 1849.

[35] *Consciousness in Concord,* ed. by Perry Miller (Boston, 1956), p. 160.

[36] *Ibid.,* p. 232, n. 52.   [37] T. *J.* I, p. 261.

[38] *Ibid.,* I, pp. 261-268.

[39] *Ibid.,* I, pp. 275-281.   [40] *Ibid.,* I, p. 344.

[41] Thoreau's spellings "Veeshnoo Sarma" and "Heetopades" agree with Wilkins' and not with those of H. T. Colebrooke, who also translated the same work in 1808. Colebrooke spells them "Vishnu Sarman" and "Hitopadesa." Also see T. *J.* I, p. 345.

[42] (New York, 1900), p. 145.

The Vedic passages that he quoted here were collected in 1842 and not at the time of the actual journey.

These years of Thoreau's Vedic explorations were also the years of close friendship with Emerson. In the 1840's of the nineteenth century, Thoreau was helping Emerson edit *The Dial*. Thoreau's reference to "Veeshnoo Sarma" in March 1842 could be the result of his attempts to help Emerson find an appropriate selection of "ethnical scriptures" for the July 1842, and for the January 1843 issues of *The Dial*.[43] Here, then, is an instance of Emerson and Thoreau collaborating on making selections from Vedic literature to which they wanted to give currency in America. Though the publication of these representative Vedic selections came in 1842 and 1843,[44] the initial attempts at gleaning those selections began in 1840. But prior to 1840, there is absolutely no evidence in any of Thoreau's journals of the nature of his early interest in Vedic literature and Vedantic philosophy.

The publication of *The Dial* in 1840 obliged Emerson and Thoreau to examine methodically the available Vedic literature. In spite of all the wealth of this literature which had been available in English, French, and German translations and critical estimates since 1785 in the works of Jones, Wilkins, Colebrooke, Anquetil-Duperron, the Abbè Dubois, Carey, Marshman, Ward, and Roy, they waited till 1840 to "plunge" deeply and enthusiastically into its study. This was the culmination of a long, gradual process in the dissemination of Vedic literature and proliferation of Vedantic ideas in America. *The Dial* became a vehicle for Emerson and Thoreau to present to their readers their "discovery" of Vedic literature. It must also be noted that by 1840 they were just developing a mature eclectic outlook towards Vedic literature and Vedantic philosophy, so that by July 1842 they were able to write: "We commence in this present number the printing of a series of selections from the oldest ethical and religious writings of men, exclusive of the Hebrew and Greek scriptures."[45] This is definite proof that during 1840-42, Emerson and Thoreau were developing into universalists very much like their mentor Sir William Jones.

---

[43] "Veeshnoo Sarma," pp. 82-85; and "The Laws of Menu," pp. 331-340 respectively.

[44] *Ibid.*

[45] III, p. 82.

In the case of Walt Whitman, evidence of an early familiarity with Vedic literature is absent. Only once did he mention having read "the ancient Hindoo poems,"[46] a statement made late in 1884. Yet Whitman implies that his reading of "the ancient Hindoo poets" is an "embryonic fact" in the making of "Leaves of Grass" which was first published in 1855. Neither in his *Specimen Days,* nor in his correspondence, nor even in the numerous notebooks he kept prior to the publication of "Leaves of Grass," does he mention any items of Vedic literature or Vedantic philosophy.[47] It may not mean that he was unaware of Vedic literature and its philosophical teachings. In fact, he summarizes his encounter with Vedic literature during October-November 1857; "India represents meditation, oriental rhapsody, passiveness, *a curious schoolmaster-teaching of wise precepts* [italics mine] . . . ."[48] Indeed, "a curious schoolmaster teaching of wise precepts" may be an allusion to "Heetopades" of "Veeshnoo Sarma" and "The Laws of Menu" which show that he read *The Dial* of July 1842 and January 1843. The notebook entry was made by Whitman in 1857, two years after the first edition of "Leaves of Grass." In the 1855 edition, only one allusion to "Brahma" occurs.[49] In its context, this allusion indicates that Whitman is aware of the Vedantic concept of the all-inclusive *Brahman.* Beyond that we have no evidence of the exact process through which Whitman derived his Vedantic ideas. Yet, by 1840's, well before Whitman became a recognized poet, Vedantic ideas were readily available, if only in the literary and intellectual climate as is evidenced by the numerous journals and

[46] "A Backward Glance O'er Travel'd Roads," in *Walt Whitman's Leaves of Grass and Selected Prose,* ed. by Sculley Bradley (New York, 1960), p. 481.

[47] *Walt Whitman: Prose Works* 1892, ed. by Floyed Stovall, I (New York, 1961); *Walt Whitman: The Early Poems and Fiction,* ed. by Thomas L. Brasher (New York, 1963); *Walt Whitman: The Correspondence* (1842-1847), ed. by Edwin E. Miller, I (New York, 1963); *Walt Whitman Workshop,* ed. by Clifton J. Furness (New York, 1928); *The Complete Prose Works of Walt Whitman,* ed. by Richard M. Bucke, *et al.* Vols. I-VII (New York and London; R. P. Putnam's Sons, 1902).

[48] *The Complete Prose Works of Walt Whitman,* ed. by Richard M. Bucke, *et al.,* Vol. VI (New York and London, 1902), pp. 103-104.

[49] *Walt Whitman's Leaves of Grass: His Original Edition,* ed. by Malcolm Cowley (New York, 1961), p. 71.

periodicals that reviewed and discussed Vedic literature and Vedantic philosophy.[50]

Thus we are led once again to believe that Emerson, Thoreau, and Whitman, to varying degrees, were interested in Vedic literature but that they did not approach it with the interest and zeal of British Sanskrit scholars like Jones and Wilkins. Therefore, prior to 1840, they were only reading about Vedic literature from secondary sources in the scholarly periodicals of their time and in some of the first English translations of Vedic literature. Their grasp of Vedantic philosophy, or even their discovery of an analogous transcendentalism in *Vedanta,* as of 1840, was still elementary. But in 1840, after they discovered "Heetopades" and "The Laws of Menu," Emerson and Thoreau accepted Vedic literature as part of their universal human heritage. And they wanted to popularize in America this newly discovered literature. So they began to read this literature carefully, with the result that they opened a new feature in *The Dial* and called it "ethnical scriptures."

Walt Whitman, however, reveals no comparable early interest. He did not even take the trouble to comment on or make notes about any encounters with Vedic literature prior to 1840. His numerous notebooks on his reading are to be found in the sixth and seventh volumes of *The Complete Prose Works of Walt Whitman* edited under the general direction of Richard M. Bucke. Bucke believes that "These notes, cuttings etc., extend from the forties down to the fifties."[51] This leaves us to conclude that before 1840, Whitman was not interested in Vedic literature and Vedantic philosophy.

Though all three chief American transcendentalists were uniquely different personalities, they had one thing in common. They were intensely individualistic. Their individualism bears close resemblance to Brahmanic supermanlike individualism.[52] Their personalities meet the description of superman according to Nietzsche as well, R. J. Hollingdale summarizes the concept as follows: "A 'Superman' is a man who has 'overcome' man —

---

[50] See Chapter 5, pp. 86-91 of this book.
[51] (New York, 1902), p. xv.
[52] See Chapter I, p. 22 of this book.

that is, himself."[53]   But they did not derive this universal individualism from their early readings in Vedic literature.   One is led to opine that as they gradually became familiar with Vedanta, in a rather normal way for persons like themselves, they faced confirmation for the direction their minds and sensibilities were taking.   Their interests intensified in 1840 and by 1842 they found *The Dial* a practical means to propagate their recently reinforced transcendental-Vedantic ideas through "ethnical scriptures". Vedanta is only one, though an important one, of the systems of transcendental philosophy that the chief American transcendentalists responded to since 1840.

In their zeal to spread their eclecticism, they showed a breadth of vision that went beyond the European heritage of American literature and thought.   Their eclecticism also led them, in an elementary way by 1840, and in a more intensified way after 1840, towards integrating their Judeo-Christian and Americo-European transcendental ideas with Hindu-Vedantic ideas.   The result of such an integration is the extensive appeal their writings now have all over the world.

[53] R. J. Hollingdale transl., *Nietzsche: Thus Spoke Zarathustra* (Baltimore, Md., 1968), p. 23.

APPENDIX

The following is a checklist of works and translations by early Sanskritists. Special care is taken in listing American editions of some of these works and translations of Vedic literature. I have enumerated the libraries which have held copies of these books and in some cases have been able to supply accession dates. I have included also histories of philosophies and surveys of literature which referred to Vedantic philosophy and Vedic literature. Much of this information came from: *Evans Index of Early American Imprints; Union Catalogue of the Library of Congress; Union List of Printed Indic Texts and Translations in American Libraries;* a few catalogues of private collections; and a limited personal research in the libraries in Philadelphia. I have taken care to include only those works which were available in America prior to 1840. Therefore, I excluded the Cholmondeley Collection which did not reach Boston till November 1855.

In listing the libraries which hold some of these Vedic texts, I hope to suggest the extent of their popularity. Besides, a checklist like the following one could be a helpful reference source for further research in accession histories of Vedic texts such as we have on the Cholmondeley Collection.

In the case of Sir William Jones, I included a checklist of his legal works as well, in support of the argument of the third chapter of this book, i.e., his American reputation as a jurist and as a supporter of American Independence led some people to take interest in his later Sanskrit researches and translations. I grouped these Sanskritists first by their nationality and next by their dates of birth.

BRITISH SANSKRITISTS

Sir William Jones (1746-1794)

(a) American editions of the life and works of Sir William Jones suggesting his popularity in America as a jurist:

1. *Memoirs of the Life,* Writings and Correspondence of Sir William Jones (first published in London. 1804) 2nd printing, Philadelphia. William Poyntell and Company, 1805.

2. *An Essay on the Law of Bailments* (first published in London: C. Dilly, 1781).

   i. Boston: Samuel Etheridge, 1796. Thomas Jefferson owned

a copy of this edition. See the *Catalogue of the Library of Thomas Jefferson,* Vol. II, p. 39.

ii.   Philadelphia: P. Byrne, 1804. Has introductory remarks and notes by John Balmanno.

iii. Albany, N. Y.: Backus and Whiting, 1806.

iv.   Brattleboro, Vt.: William Fessenden, 1807.

v.   Brattleboro, Vt.: William Fessenden, 1813.

vi.   New York: D. Halsted, 1828 with notes and references to American decisions by William Halsted, Jr.

vii. Philadelphia: Hogan & Thompson, 1836.

3.   "Select Poems of Sir William Jones: With a Life of the Author," *The Works of the British Poets,* ed. by Robert Walsh, Vol. XXXV, Philadelphia: Samuel F. Bradford, 1822.

(b) Non-American editions of the life and works of Sir William Jones found in American libraries:

1.   i.   *The Works of Sir William Jones,* London: G. G. and J. Robinson, 1799, ed. by Anna Marie Jones, 6 vols. Two supplementary volumes issued in 1801 contain the first five volumes of *Asiatick Researches* minus those writings of Jones which are already in the *Works.*

Copies at: American Oriental Society (Yale University), Emory University Library, Harvard University Library, Huntington Library (San Marino), Library of Congress, Northwestern University Library, University of Hawaii Library, University of Texas Library, Yale University Library, University of Pennsylvania Library, Library Company of Philadelphia, Wagner Institute Library, Bryn Mawr College Library, Longwood College Library, American Philosophical Society Library (Philadelphia).

ii.   London: J. Stockdale, 1807, in 13 volumes, includes all of Jones's writings plus Lord Teignmouth's *Memoirs.*

Copies at: Cleveland Public Library, Harvard University Library, Union Theological Seminary (New York), U. S. Military Academy Library, University of Illinois Library, University of Texas Library, Temple University Library, Haverford College Library, Penn State University Library, Academy of New Church (Bryn Athyn) Library.

2.   i.   *Memoirs of the Life,* writings and correspondence of Sir William Jones, by Lord Teignmouth, London: J. Hatchard, 1804.

Copies at: Harvard University Library, Library of Congress, Oberlin College Library, University of South Carolina Library, University of Pennsylvania, American Philosophical Society Library.

ii. Philadelphia: William Poyntell and Company, 1805.

Copies at: American Antiquarian Society (Worcester, Mass)., Boston Public Library, Harvard University Library, Library of Congress, Ohio State University Library, Princeton University Library, Stanford University Library, Union Theological Seminary (New York), University of Hawaii Library, University of Pennsylvania Library, American Philosophical Society Library.

iii. London: J. Bretell, 1896, 2 vols.

Copies at: Library of Congress, Peabody Institute (Baltimore), U. S. Department of State Library, University of Texas Library.

iv. London: John Hatchard, Second edition. 1806.

Copies at: American Oriental Society (Yale University), Library of Congress, Peabody Institute (Baltimore), Public Library of Cleveland, University of Hawaii Library, University of Rochester Library, Yale University Library.

v. London: J. Hatchard, New edition, 1807.

Copies at: Library of Congress, New York City Library, Princeton University Library, Western Reserve University Library.

vi. London: J. Hatchard, Sixth edition, 1815.

Copies at: Harvard Medical School Library, Newberry Library (Chicago), New York City Public Library, Union Theological Seminary Library (New York).

3. i. *Poems,* Consisting Chiefly of Translations from the Asiatick Languages, Oxford: Clarendon Press, 1772.

Copies at: Boston Public Library, Harvard University Library, Princeton University Library, Public Library of Cleveland, University of Chicago Library, University of Illinois Library, University of Michigan Library, University of Wisconsin Library, Yale University Library.

ii. London: W. Boyer and J. Nichols, Second edition, 1777.

Copies at: Lehigh University Library, Newberry Library (Chicago), Public Library of Cleveland, University of Illinois Library, University of North Carolina Library, Library Company of Philadelphia.

4. i. "Select Poems of Sir William Jones: with a Life of the Author,"

The Works of the British Poets, ed. by Robert Walsh, Vol. XXXV, Philadelphia: Samuel F. Bradford, 1822.

The editor Robert Walsh was a versatile scholar who was professor of English at the University of Pennsylvania from 1818-28. Between 1822-23 he edited the *Museum of Foreign Literature and Science.* From 1827-37, he edited *The American Quarterly Review.* The reliable guess is that his fifty volume set of *The Works of the British Poets,* being the first of its kind in America, was available in every College Library and was read by every student of literature since 1822. Volume thirty-five of this set is devoted to the "Life and Poems of Sir William Jones," pp. 3-242.

5.   i.   "An Ode in Imitation of Alcaeus" was the most popular anthology piece. Besides appearing in such anthologies as Walsh's, it also appeared on broadsides. The Library Company of Philadelphia has a broadside of this poem but there is no history of its accession.

     ii. The same Ode also appears in a bound volume of Political Pamphlets in the Loganian Library. The pamphlets are related to some controversy between the Old and the New Whigs. Its appearance in this collection is, perhaps, an implied recognition of the philosophy of natural rights the Ode seems to espouse. The Ode seems to have been in Loganian Library since 1811 according to the date on the book plate. It has been transferred to the Library Company of Philadelphia.

6.   i.   *The Principles of Government,* in a dialogue between a Scholar and a Peasant, London, 1782. This was anonymously Published by the Society for Constitutional Information.

Copies at: Library of Congress (This copy was owned by Thomas Jefferson. See *Catalogue of The Library of Thomas Jefferson,* Vol. II, p. 146). Western Reserve Historical Society.

     ii. London: C. Dilly, 1792, acknowledges the authorship of Sir William, Jones, Is found in a collection of Whig pamphlets ed. by W. Belsham, *Examination of an Appeal from the New to the Old Whigs.* The volume has been in the Loganian Library since 1811.

     iii. London, 1818.

Copies at: Princeton University Library, Yale University Library.

7.   i.   *The Muse Recalled,* an Ode, On the Nuptials of Lord Viscount

Althorp and Miss Lavinia Bingham, eldest daughter of Charles Lord Lucan, March 6, 1781, Paris: Franc Ambr. Didot L'Aine, 1781.

Copies at: Harvard University Library, University of Illinois (Urbana) Library, Duke University Library, Boston Public Library, Princeton University Library, Folger Shakespeare Library (Washington, D. C.).

ii. Strawberry-Hill Twickingham, S. Middlesex, England, 1782.

Copies at: Library Company of Philadelphia (bound in a volume of political pamphlets once owned by Benjamin Franklin), American Philosophical Society Library (bound in a volume of political pamphlets "belonging originally to Benjamin Franklin" and presented to the Society by John Vaughan on October 3, 1828. The popularity in America is understandable because it contains a denunciation of tyranny and expresses the brightest hopes for America. The appropriate lines have been quoted in the body of the third chapter. These copies probably attest more to the friendship and mutual admiration of Franklin and Jones than to Jones's reputation as a poet).

8. i. *A Grammar of Persian Language,* London: W. A. J. Richardson, 1771.

Copies at: University of Michigan Library, Yale University Library, Charleston College Library (in the collection of James Warley Miles. The Collection was deposited in 1854).

ii. London: Richardson, 1775.

Copies at: Public Library of Cleveland: American Philosophical Society Library (presented by John Vaughan who did not take a scholarly interest in Oriental languages).

iii. London: J. Murray, 1783.

Copies at: Princeton University Library, Yale University Library.

iv. London: J. Murray & S. Highley, 1801.

Copies at: Boston Public Library, Harvard University Library, Hebrew Union College Library (Cincinnati), Princeton University Library, Public Library of Cleveland, Tufts College Library, Yale University Library.

v. London: Lackington, Allen, and Company, 1809.

Copies at: Boston Public Library, Hebrew Union College Library (Cincinnati), Library of Congress, Yale University Library.

9.   i.   *Dissertations and Miscellaneous Pieces* ... by Sir William Jones, *et al.,* 2 Vols., London: Nichol, 1792, University of Michigan; Yale University Library; University of Chicago; Lee University Library, Va., Swarthmore College Library.

    ii.   *Dissertations and Miscellaneous Pieces,* Relating to the History and Antiquities, the Arts, Sciences and Literature of Asia, by Sir William Jones, *et al.,* 2 Vols., the first consisting entirely of Jones's writings, Dublin: P. Byrne, 1793.

Copies at: The University of Pensylvania Library, Library Company of Philadelphia, American Philosophical Society Library, Lutheran Theological Seminary (Phila., Pa.), Swarthmore College Library, Library of Congress; University of Kentucky Library; University of Texas Library; Duke University Library; University of Illinois, Urbana; Northwestern University Library, Allegheny College Library, Meadville, Pa.

10.   i.   *Poeseos Asiaticae Commentorum* ... cum Appendice, London, 1774.

Copies at: The University of Pennsylvania Library, Library Company of Philadelphia, American Philosophical Society Library, Lutheran Theological Seminary (Philadelphia, Pa.), Library of Congress (Thomas Jefferson Library).

    ii.   London: Lipsiae, 1777.

Copies at: Bryn Mawr College Library.

11.   i.   *The Literary History of the Late Sir William Jones, in a Discourse,* by Sir John Shore/Lord Teignmouth, London: Edward Jeffery 1795.

Copies at: American Philosophical Society Library.

12.   i.   *Asiatic Miscellany,* ed. by W. Chamber and Sir William Jones, 2 Vols., Calcutta, 1785-1786.

Copies at: Library Company of Philadelphia (imperfect), University of Michigan Library, Harvard University Library, University of Chicago Library.

    ii.   *Asiatic Miscellany,* Consisting of Transactions, Imitations, Fugitive Pieces, Original Productions, and Extracts from

Curious Publications, by W. Chambers & Sir W. Jones, London: J. Wallis, 1787.

Copies at: Library Company of Philadelphia (This copy was purchased for the Company from James Cox, an artist of the City of Philadelphia), Bryn Mawr College Library, Duke University Library, Yale University Library, Cornell University Library, Newberry Library (Chicago), Allegheny College (Meadville, Pa.), Johns Hopkins University Library.

13. i. *Sacontala;* or, the Fatal Ring: An Indian Drama by Calidasa, translated from the original Sanscrit and Pracrit by Sir William Jones, London, 1792.

Copies at: Library Company of Philadelphia; Library of Congress (Thomas Jefferson); Harvard University Library; Cleveland Public Library.

ii. ———— in *Works,* VI, pp. 201-312.

14. i. *Asiatick Researches*; or, Transactions of the Society Instituted in Bengal, 4 Vols. ed. by Sir William Jones and also issued as Supplements to his *Works* in 1801, Calcutta, 1788-94.

Copies at: American Philosophical Society (all four volumes acquired on November 2, 1804).

ii. *Asiatic Researches,* 5 Vols., London: P. Elmsley, 1798-1799.

Copies at: The University of Pennsylvania Library (five volumes in the Founders' Collection have been catalogued first in 1829), Academy of Natural Science Library (Phila., Pa.), Philadelphia Free Library, Library of Congress.

iii. 6 Vols., London: Sewell, 1801, has the same pagination as the Calcutta edition.

Copies at: American Philosophical Society Library (The title sheet has a note in ink reading, "American Philosophical Society, Philadelphia, 4 Dec., 1801. Presented by Sam F. Bradford." On this occasion Bradford had made a speech to the Society in which he referred to Jones in admiration for his love of independence and scholarship in Oriental Literature), German Society Library.

iv. 11 Vols., London: Vernon, 1806-12.

Copies at: University of Pennsylvania Music Library, Library Co. of Philadelphia, Dropsie College Library, Franklin Institute Library, Swarthmore College Library.

v. 12 Vols., London, 1801-1818.

Copies at: Swarthmore College Library, American Philosophical Society Library (Philadelphia, Pa.), Penn State University Library.

15. i. *Institutes of Hindu Law; or, The Ordinances of Menu, According to the Gloss of Culluca* ... Calcutta: By Order of the Government, 1794.

Copies at: Columbia University Library; Harvard University.

ii. ———— with a Preface by Sir William Jones ... London: J. Sewell, 1796.

Copies at: New York Public Library; Boston Public Library.

iii. ———— in *Works,* VII, pp. 73-399.

Copies at: New York Public Library; Boston Public Library.

16. i. "Hitopadesa, or the Salutary Instruction of Vishnu Sarman ..." *Works,* XIII, pp. 1-210. Not to be confused with translations of the same by Charles Wilkins and H. T. Colebrooke.

Copies at: New York Public Library; Boston Public Library.

Broughton, Thomas D. (1778-1835)

1. i. *Selections from the Popular Poetry of the Hindus,* London: John Marton, 1814 (a collection of folk songs in Hindi on verso and English Trans. on recto).

Copies at: Library of Congress; Princeton University Library; Harvard University Library; Brown University Library; New York Public Library; Columbia University Library.

Colebrooke, H. T. (1765-1837)

1. i. Trans. *A Digest of Hindu Law on Contracts and Successions,* 3 vols., London, 1801.

Copies at: Library Company of Philadelphia.

ii. *A Digest of Hindu Law* ..., 4 vols., Calcutta: Hon'ble Co. Press, 1797-1798.

Copies at: New York Public Library.

2. *A Grammar of the Sanscrita Language,* I, Calcutta: Hon'ble Co. Press, 1805, xxii, 399 pp.
   Copies at: University of Pennsylvania Library; Academy of New Church Library (Bryn Athyn).
3. *Remarks on the International Husbandry and Commerce of Bengal* ..., London, 1806.
   Copies at: Library Company of Philadelphia.
4. "On the Vedas, or the Sacred Writings of the Hindus", in *Asiatic Researches; or, Transactions of the Society Instituted in Bengal* ..., vol. VIII (London, 1808), pp. 377-497.
   Copies at: University of Pennsylvania; Library Company of Philadelphia; Lutheran Theological Seminary of Philadelphia.
5. *Amarakosa,* Serampore: Mission Press, 1808, vii, 217 pp.
   Copies at: University of Pennsylvania Library.
6. *Hitopadesa* ..., Serampore: Mission Press, 1804.
   Copies at: Library of Congress.
7. *Hitopadesa,* Dunstable: J. W. Morris, 1808.
   Copies at: Library of Congress.
8. *Obligations and Contracts,* London, 1818.
   Copies at: University of Pennsylvania Library.
9. *Miscellaneous Essays,* 2 vols., London: W. H. Allen & Co., 1837.
   Copies at: Library Company of Philadelphia.
10. *Essays on The Religion and Philosophy of the Hindus* (reprinted from learned journals), London: Williams and Norgate, 1837.
    Copies at: Yale University Library; Library of Congress; Cleveland Public Library; Harvard University Library; Library Company of Philadelphia.

Wilson, Horace H. (1786-1860)

1. *Select Specimens of the Theatre of the Hindus,* trans. 3 vols., Calcutta, 1827.
   Copies at: American Philosophical Society Library.
2. ——— 2nd edn., London: Parbury & Allen & Co., 1835.
   Copies at: Free Library of Philadelphia; University of Pennsylvania; Library Company of Philadelphia.
3. *A Dictionary in Sanscrit and English,* Calcutta: 2nd edn., 1832.
   Copies at: University of Pennsylvania Library; Library Company of Philadelphia.
4. *Vishnu Purana,* London: Oriental Translation Fund, 1840.
   Copies at: Library Company of Philadelphia.
5. *Essays and Lectures Chiefly on the Religion of the Hindus,* 2 vols., London: Trubner & Co., 1862.
   Copies at: University of Pennsylvania Library; Historical Society of Pennsylvania.
6. *Megha Doota;* or *Cloud Messenger,* Calcutta: College of Fort William, 1813.

Copies at: Yale University Library; Johns Hopkins Library; Library of Congress; Harvard University Library.

Wilkins, Charles (1749-1836)

1. *Sanskrit Grammar,* Calcutta, 1779.
   Copies at: Library of Congress.
2. *Bhagavat-Geeta,* or dialogues of Kreeshna and Arjoon ..., London: C. Nourse, 1785.
   Copies at: Yale University Library; New York Public Library; Harvard University Library; Boston Public Library.
3. *Heetopades of Veeshnoo-Sarma,* Bath (England): Gruttwell, 1787, 334 pp.
   Copies at: University of Pennsylvania Library; Bryn Mawr College Library; Library Company of Philadelphia; Rosenwald Collection, Jenkintown, Pa.; New York Public Library; Princeton University Library; Cleveland Public Library; Harvard University Library.

Carey, William (1761-1836)

1. *Dialogues; Intended to Facilitate the Acquiring of the Bengalee Language,* Serampore [Mission Press], 1801.
   Copies at: University of Pennsylvania (acquired before 1829), bears the inscription "Presented by the Rev. William Carey, D. D., To the University of Pennsylvania"; Library Company of Philadelphia.
2. *Grammar of the Bengalee Language,* Serampore: Mission, n.d.
   Copies at: Library Company of Philadelphia.
3. ———— Serampore: Mission Press, 4th edn., 1818.
   Copies at: University of Pennsylvania Library.
4. *The Ramayana* ..., Dunstable: J. W. Morris, 1808.
   Copies at: New York Public Library.
5. *A Grammar of the Mahratta Language* ..., Serampore: Mission Press, 1805.
   Copies at: University of Pennsylvania Library.
6. ————-, Serampore: Mission Press, 2nd ed., 1808, 157 pp.
   Copies at: American Philosophical Library of Philadelphia.
7. *Grammar of the Sungskrit Language,* Serampore: Mission Press, 1806.
   Copies at: University of Pennsylvania acquired before 1829; American Philosophical Library of Philadelphia; New York Public Library.
8. *A Grammar of Punjabee Language,* Serampore: Mission Press, 1812.
   Copies at: University of Pennsylvania Library.
9. *A Grammar of the Telinga Language,* Serampore: Mission Press, 1814.
   Copies at: University of Pennsylvania Library.
10. *A Dictionary of Bengalee Language...,* 3 vols., Serampore; Mission Press, 1818-1825.
    Copies at: American Philosophical Library of Philadelphia.
11. *The Dying peasant and other Poems . . .,* Philadelphia: H. C. Carey, 1826, viii, 160 pp.

Copies at: University of Pennsylvania Library; Library Company of Philadelphia; Athenaeum of Philadelphia.

Ward, William (1769-1823)

1. *Account of the Writings, Religion, and Manners of the Hindoos,* 4 vols., Serampore: Mission Press, 1811.
   Copies at: University of Pennsylvania Library.

2. *A View of the History, Literature, and Mythology of the Hindoos; including a Minute Description of the Manners and Customs, and Translations from their Principal Works,* 2 vols., Serampore: Mission Press, 1818.
   Copies at: Lutheran Theological Seminary (Philadelphia); American Philosophical Society (Philadelphia); Philadelphia Free Library; American Baptist Historical Society (Philadelphia); Historical Society of Pennsylvania.

3. *Farewell Letters to Britain and America on Returning to Bengal,* Lexington, Ky.: Skillman, 1822.
   Copies at: Presbyterian Historical Society (Philadelphia, Pa.).

GERMAN SANSKRITISTS

Ritter, Heinrich (1791-1869)

1. *The History of Ancient Philosophy,* 4 vols., Oxford, 1804.
   Copies at: University of Pennsylvania Library.

2. *Geschichte der Philosophie,* 8 vols., Hamburg: Friedrich Perthes, 1829, refers to Colebrooke vol. i, pp. 94, 113, 430, 439, 550; and to Jones in vol. VII, p. 280, vol. VIII, p. 487.
   Copies at: University of Pennsylvania Library.

3. *The History of Ancient Philosophy,* trans. into English by J. W. Morrison, Oxford: D. A. Tolboys, 1837.
   Copies at: University of Pennsylvania Library.

4. *Histoire de la Philosophie,* trans. into French, C. J. Tissot, 8 vols., Paris: Librarire de Language [?], 1835. (The information on Vedanta in Vol. II, pp. 53-120 is more thorough than in De Gerando's *History of Philosophy.*)
   Copies at: University of Pennsylvania Library.

Wagner, Udolph (1774-1833)

1. *John Arnold Kanne's System der Indischen Mythe,* oder Chronus und die Geschichte de Gottmenschen im der Periode des Vorruckens der Nachtgleichen, Leipzig: Wengandschen Buchhandlung, 1815.
   Copies at: Academy of New Church Library (Bryn Athyn).

HINDU SANSKRITISTS

Roy, Rammohun (1774-1833)

1. *Translation of the Ishopanishad...*, Calcutta: Hindoostanee Press, 1816.
   Copies at: Cleveland Public Library; Harvard University Library.
2. *Translation of Several Principal Books ... Of the Veds*, London: Parbury, Allen, 1832.
   Copies at: Yale University Library; Princeton University Library; Library of Congress; New York Public Library; University of Pennsylvania Library.

MISCELLANEOUS BRITISH AND AMERICAN WRITERS

1. Terry, Edward (Chaplain to Sir Thomas Rowe) *A Voyage to East India...*, London: J. Wilkie, 1777.
   Copies at: University of Pennsylvania Library.

Callcott, Lady Maria (1785-1842)

1. *Letters on India,* London: Hurst, Rees, Orme, and Browne, 1808.
   Copies at: Library of Congress.
2. ————— 2nd edn., London: Longman, 1814, 382 pp.
   Copies at: University of Pennsylvania; Library Company of Philadelphia.
3. *Journal of Residence in India,* Edinburgh: G. Ramsay, 1812, vii, 211.
   Copies at: Library of Congress.

Heber, Bishop Reginold (1783-1826)

1. *Narrative of Journey through the Upper Provinces of India...*, 2 vols., Philadelphia: Carey, Lea & Carey, 1828.
   Copies at: This being the first American edition, it may be safe to assume that copies of this edition were acquired by several libraries in the country.

Murray, Hugh (1779-1846), *et al.*

1. *Historical and Descriptive Account of British India...*, New York: J. & J. Harper, 1832. Was issued in the Harper's Family Library Series.
   Copies at: At almost all the major U. S. Libraries and private collections.

Caunter, Hobart (1794-1851)

1. *The Oriental Annual,* or *Scenes from India,* 2 vols., London: Bull and Churton, 1834-1835.

Copies at: University of Pennsylvania Library; New York Public Library.

2. ———— New Series, vol. I, Philadelphia: Desilver, Thomas & Co., 1837.
Copies at: All major American Libraries.

Bacon, Thomas (1813-1892)

1. ed. *Oriental Annual Containing a Series of Tales, Legends, & Historical Romances.* Philadelphia: Carey and Hart, 1840.
Copies at: All major U. S. Libraries.

AMERICAN MISSIONARY REPORTS

1. *Annual Report of the American Board of Commissioners for Foreign Missions,* Boston, 1810.
Copies at: All the Seminaries, and major U. S. Libraries.
2. *The Baptist Mission in India,* Philadelphia: Hellings and Aiken, 1811.
Copies at: Seminaries and major U. S. Libraries.

FRENCH SANSKRITISTS

Anquetil-Duperron, A. H. (1731-1805)

1. *Legislation Orientale,* ouvrages dans lequel, en montrant quels sont en Turquil, en Parse et dans l'Indoustan . . . Amsterdam: MM. Ray, 1778.
Copies at: University of Pennsylvania Library; New York Public Library.
2. *L'Inde en Rapport avec l'Europe . . .* 2 vols., Paris: Moutardier, 1799.
Copies at: Academy of New Church Library (Bryn Athyn, Pa.); University of Pennsylvania Library.
3. *Oupnek'hat* (id est, secretum tegendum) . . . 2 vols., Paris: Levrault, 1801, 1802.
Copies at: Academy of New Church Library; New York Public Library; Library of Congress.
4. *Versuch* einer neuen darstellung der uralten indischen all-eins lehre . . . [an abridged translation of Duperron's *Oupnek'hat*] by Thaddae Anselm Rixner, Nurnberg: Steinischen buchhandlung, 1808.
Copies at: Academy of New Church Library.

Degerando, Joseph Marie (1772-1842)

1. i. *Histoire Compareé des Systèmes de Philosophie,* 4 vols., Paris: Alexis Eymery, 1804.
Copies at: University of Pennsylvania Library.

ii. ————, 2 vols., Paris: 2nd edn., Alexis Eymery, 1822-1823. Copies at: Library of Congress.

Langlois, S. A. (1788-1854)

1.　i. *Harivansa;* ou histoire de la famille de Hari ..., 2 vols., Paris, 1834 ———— and London, 1835.
Copies at: Yale University Library; Cleveland Public Library; University of Pennsylvania Library; Princeton University Library; University of Chicago Library; Harvard University Library; Boston Museum of Fine Arts Library; Boston Public Library.

Dubois, The Abbè J. A. (1765-1848)

1.　i. *Description of the Character ... of the People of India,* 2 vols., London: East India Company, 1817.
Copies at: Library of Congress.
　　ii. ————, Philadelphia: Carey, 1818 (American Edn.).
Copies at: Major Seminaries and University Libraries in America.
2.　i. *Le Pantcha-Tantra,* on les Cinqi Ruses, fables du Brahme Vichnou-Sarman; Adventures de Paramartha, et autres contes, le tout tradiet pour la primiro foix sur les originaux indiens par ... J. A. Dubois, Paris: J. S. Merlin, 1826.
Copies at: New York Public Library.

Lassen, Christian (1800-1876)

1.　ed. *Anthologia Sanscritica* :..., Bonnae, 1830.
Copies at: University of Pennsylvania Library; Lutheran Theological Seminary (Philadelphia).
2.　*Gitagovinda Jayadevae poetae indici drama lyricum,* Bonnae, 1836.
Copies at: Yale University Library; American Oriental Society Library; Columbia University Library; New York Public Library; Johns Hopkins University Library; Library of Congress; Princeton University Library; University of Chicago Library; McGill University Library; Harvard University Library.

SELECTED BIBLIOGRAPHY

ALLEN, GAY W. *The Solitary Singer*: *A Critical Biography of Walt Whitman*. New York: The Macmillan Co., 1955.

————. ed. *Walt Whitman Abroad*. Syracuse: Syracuse University Press, 1955.

"A Metaphysician" (pseudonym). "Emerson Poet and Philosopher." *Indian Review*, LX (August 1959), 404-405.

ARBER, AGNES. *The Manifold and the One*. London: John Murray, 1957.

ASSELINEAU, ROGER. *The Evolution of Walt Whitman*. 2 vols. Cambridge, Mass: The Belknap Press of Harvard University Press, 1962.

BAIRD, JAMES. *Ishmael*. Baltimore: Johns Hopkins Press, 1956.

BEARD, CHARLES A., and MARY R. *The American Spirit*: *A Study of the Idea of Civilization in the United States*. New York: The Macmillan Co., 1942.

Biographie Universelle (Michaud): *Ancienne et Moderne*. Paris: Novelle Edition, n.d.

BISHOP, JONATHAN. *Emerson on the Soul*. Cambridge, Mass.: Harvard University Press, 1964.

BLAU, JOSEPH L., ed. *American Philosophical Addresses* 1700-1900. New York: Columbia University Press, 1946.

BRADLEY, SCULLEY. "The Fundamental Metrical Principle of Whitman's Poetry." *American Literature*, X (January 1939), 437-459.

BRAHAM, LIONEL. "Emerson and Boehme: A Comparative Study in Mystical Ideas." *Modern Language Quarterly*, XX (March 1959), 31-35.

BRAITHWAITE, WILLIAM C. *The Beginnings of Quakerism*. Cambridge, England: Cambridge University Press, 1955.

BRIDGMAN, RICHARD. "The Meaning of Emerson's Title, 'Hamatreya.'" *Emerson Society Quarterly*, II Quarter (1962), 16.

BROOKS, VAN WYCK. *The Flowering of New England*. New York: E. P. Dutton & Co., 1952.

————. *The Life of Emerson*. New York: E. P. Dutton & Co., 1932.

BROWN, STUART G. "Emerson's Platonism." *New England Quarterly*, XVIII (September 1945), 325-345.

BRYANT, WILLIAM C. "A Review of Rammohan Roy's 'Precepts of Jesus'" *New York Review and Athenaeum Magazine*, I (June 1825), 442-453.

BUCKE, RICHARD M., ed. *Cosmic Consciousness*: *A Study in the Evolution of the Human Mind*. Philadelphia: Innes and Sons, 1901.

————. *Memories of Walt Whitman*. Philadelphia: Walt Whitman Fellowship, 1894.

————. "Portraits of Walt Whitman." *New England Quarterly,* XX (March 1890), 34-50.

BURCH, GEORGE B. "The Hindu Concept of Existence." *The Monist,* L (1960), 44-54.

CAMERON, KENNETH W. "More Notes on Orientalism in Emerson's Harvard." *Emerson Society Quarterly,* I Quarter (1961), 81-90.

————. *Ralph Waldo Emerson's Reading.* Raleigh, N. C.: The Thistle Press, 1941.

CADY EDWIN H. *John Woolman: The Mind of a Quaker Saint.* New York: Washington Square Press, 1966.

CAMERON, KENNETH W., ed. *Transcendental Climate: New Resources for the Study of Emerson, Thoreau, and their Contemporaries.* 3 vols. Hartford, Conn.: Transcendental Books, 1963.

CAMPBELL, HENRY M. "Emerson and Whitehead." *PMLA,* LXXV (December 1960), 577-582.

CANNON, GARLAND. *Oriental Jones.* New York: Asia Publishing House, 1964.

————. "Sir William Jones and Benjamin Franklin." (Oxford) *University College Record,* IV (October 1961), 27-45.

CARPENTER, FREDERIC I. "American Transcendentalism in India (1961)." *Emerson Society Quarterly* (II Quarter 1963), 59-62.

————. *Emerson and Asia.* Cambridge, Mass.: Harvard University Press, 1930.

————. *Emerson Handbook.* New York: Hendricks House Inc., 1953.

CHAITANYA, KRISHNA. *A New History of Sanskrit Literature.* New York: Asia Publishing House, 1962.

CHAKRAVARTI, S. C. *The Philosophy of the Upanishads.* Calcutta: University of Calcutta Press, 1935.

CHALMERS, ALEXANDER, ed. *The General Biographical Dictionary.* London: New Edition, J. Nichols and Son, 1812.

CHANDRASEKHARAN, K. R. "Emerson's 'Brahma:' An Indian Interpretation." *New England Quarterly,* XXXIII (December 1961), 506-512.

CHARI, V. K. "Whitman and the Christian Sensibility." *Walt Whitman Review,* VI (March 1960), 6-7.

————. *Whitman in the Light of Vedantic Mysticism.* Lincoln, Nebraska: Nebraska University Press, 1964.

CHRISTY, ARTHUR. *The Orient in American Transcendentalism: A Study of Emerson, Thoreau, and Alcott.* New York: Columbia University Press, 1932.

CLARK, HARRY H., ed. *Transitions in American Literary Thought.* Durham, N. C.: Duke University Press, 1953.

COLLET, SOPHIA D. *The Life and Letters of Rajah Rammohun Roy.* 3rd edn. Sadharan Brahmo Samaj, 1962.

COOKE, GEORGE W. *An Historical and Biographical Introduction to Accompany THE DIAL.* 2 vols. New York: Russell and Russell, 1961.

————. *Ralph Waldo Emerson. His Life, Writings, and Philosophy*. New York and Boston: Houghton, Mifflin and Co., 1900.

DASGUPTA, SURRENDRA N. *Hindu Mysticism,* New York: Friedrick Ungar Publishing Co., 1959.

DETWEILER, ROBERT. "The Over-Rated 'Over-Soul.'" *American Literature,* XXXVI (March 1964), 65-68.

DEUSSEN, PAUL. *System of Vedanta.* Translated by Charles Johnson. Chicago: The Open Court Publishing Co., 1912.

EARNEST, ERNEST. *John and William Bartram: Botanists and Explorers.* Philadelphia: University of Pennsylvania Press, 1940.

EDWARDS, JONATHAN. *Images or Shadows of Divine Things.* Edited by Perry Miller. New Haven: Yale University Press, 1948.

EISINGER, CHESTER E. "Transcendentalism: Its Effect upon American Literature." *American Renaissance,* XXX (1962), 22-38.

ELLIS, CHARLES MAYO. *An Essay on Transcendentalism* (1842). Intro. by Walter Harding. Gainsville, Florida: Scholars' Facsimiles and Reprints, 1954.

"Emerson and India." Unpublished Ph.D. dissertation by Man Mohn Singh, University of Pennsylvania, 1947.

EMERSON, EDWARD W., and FORBES, WALDO E., eds. *Journals of Ralph Waldo Emerson.* 10 vols. Cambridge, Mass.: Houghton, Mifflin and Co., 1909.

————. *The Complete Works of Ralph Waldo Emerson.* 10 vols. Boston and New York: Houghton, Mifflin and Co., 1909-1914.

EMERSON, RALPH WALDO. *The Journals and Miscellaneous Notebooks of ....* Edited by H. Gilman, *et al.* 6 vols. Cambridge, Mass.: The Belknap Press of Harvard University Press, 1960-66.

————. *The Letters of ....* Edited by Ralph L. Rusk. 6 vols. New York: Columbia University Press, 1910.

"Emerson's Poetry: A Study of Form and Techniques." Unpublished Ph. D. dissertation by Richard A. Yoder, University of Pennsylvania, 1967.

EMERSON, RALPH WALDO. *Indian Superstition.* Edited by Kenneth W. Cameron. Hanover, N. H.: 1954. Reprinted in *Emerson Society Quarterly* (1963), 1-63.

————. Excerpted. "Veeshnoo Sarma." *The Dial,* III (July 1842), 82-85.

EULERT, DONALD D. "Matter and Method: Emerson and the Way of Zen." *The East/West Review,* III (Winter 1966-67), 48-65.

EUMENEAU, M. B. *Union List of Printed India Texts and Translations in American Libraries.* New Haven, Conn.: American Oriental Society, 1935.

FAGIN, N. BRYLLION. *William Bartram: Interpreter of American Landscape.* Baltimore: The Johns Hopkins Press, 1933.

FISHER, GEORGE P. *Life of Benjamin Silliman.* 2 vols. New York: Charles Scribner, 1866.

FOERSTER, NORMAN. *Nature in American Literature: Studies in Modern View of Nature.* New York: Russell and Russell, 1950.

FRANKLIN, BENJAMIN. *The Complete Works of . . . .* Edited by John Bigelow. 10 Vols. New York, 1887-1889.

———. *The Works of . . . .* 10 vols. Boston, 1836-1840.

FROTHINGHAM, OCTAVIUS B. *Transcendentalism in New England: A History.* New York: Harper Torch Books, 1959.

FURNESS, CLIFTON J., ed. *Walt Whitman Workshop: A Collection of Unpublished Manuscripts.* New York: Russell and Russell, 1964.

FUSSELL, EDWIN. *The Frontier in American Literature and American West.* Princeton: Princeton University Press, 1965.

GADGIL, GANGADHAR. "Some Parallels in the Development of American and Indian Literature." *Western Humanities Review,* XVII (Spring 1963), 107-116.

GARRET, GEOFFREY T., ed. *The Legacy of India.* Oxford: The Clarendon Press, 1931.

GODDARD, HAROLD C. *Studies in New England Transcendentalism.* New York: Columbia University Press, 1908, 62-81, 126-128.

GODHES, CLARENCE L. F. *The Periodicals of American Transcendentalism.* Durham, N. C.: Duke University Press, 1931.

GONDA, J. *Notes on Brahman.* Utrecht, 1950.

GOREN, LEYLA. "Elements of Brahmanism in the Transcendentalism of Emerson." *Emerson Society Quarterly,* Supplement (I Quarter, 1964), 31-60.

GUTHRIE, WILLIAM N. *Walt Whitman: Camden Sage.* New York: Putnam's Sons, 1916.

HARDING, WALTER R. *Emerson's Library.* Charlottesville: University of Virginia Press, 1967.

———. *A Thoreau Handbook.* New York: Yale University Press, 1967.

———. *Emerson's Library.* Charlottesville: University of Virginia Press, 1967.

———. *The Days of Henry Thoreau.* New York: Alfred A. Knopf, 1965.

———. *Thoreau's Library.* Charlottesville: University of Virginia Press, 1957.

HARE, WILLIAM L. *Mysticism of East and West: Studies in Mystical and Moral Philosophy.* New York: Harcourt, Brace and Co., 1923.

HAROLD, EDWIN. *A Concordance of Walt Whitman's "Leaves of Grass and Selected Prose Writings."* Seattle: University of Washington Press, 1955.

HARRISON, JOHN S. *The Teachers of Emerson.* New York: Sturge and Walton Co., 1910.

HENDRICK, GEORGE. "Influence of Thoreau and Emerson on Gandhi's Satyagraha." *Gandhi Marg, III* (July 1959), 165-178.

————. "Whitman's Copy of *The Bhagavad Gita.*" *Walt Whitman Review,* V (March 1959), 12-14.

HINTZ, HOWARD W. *The Quaker Influence in American Literature,* London: Fleming H. Revell Co., 1940.

HIRIYANNA, M. *The Essentials of Indian Philosophy.* London: George, Allen and Unwin, 1949.

HOLLINGDALE, R. J., translator. *Nietzsche: Thus Spoke Zarathustra.* Baltimore, Md.: Penguin Classics, 1968.

HUTCHINSON, WILLIAM R. *The Transcendentalist Ministers.* New Haven: Yale University Press, 1959.

The Interpretors' Bible.

IRIE, YUKIO. "Why the Japanese People Find a Kinship with Emerson and Thoreau." *Emerson Society Quarterly* (II Quarter, 1962), 13-16.

IYENGAR, K. R. S. *Indian Writing in English.* New York: Asia Publishing House, 1962.

JAMES, WILLIAM. *The Varieties of Religious Experience.* New York: Longmans, Green and Co., 1925.

JOHNSON, JANE. "Whitman's Changing Attitude Toward Emerson." *PMLA, LXXIII* (September 1958), 452.

JONES, HOWARD MUMFORD. *Ideas in America.* Cambridge, Mass.: Harvard University Press, 1945.

KASER, DAVID. *Messrs. Carey & Lea of Philadelphia.* Philadelphia: University of Pennsylvania Press, 1957.

KWAIT, JOSEPH J. "Thoreau's Philosophical Apprenticeship." *New England Quarterly,* XVIII (March 1945), 51-69.

LATOURETTE, KENNETH S. *A History of the Expansion of Christianity.* 6 vols. New York: Harper and Bros., 1944.

LAUTER, PAUL. "Truth and Nature: Emerson's Use of Two Complex Words." *English Literary History,* XXVII (March 1960), 66-85.

"Leaves of Grass and the Bhagavad Gita: A Comparative Study." Unpublished Ph.D. dissertation by Dorothy F. Mercer, University of California, 1933.

LEIGHTON, WALTER L. *French Philosophers and New England Transcendentalism.* Charlottesville: University of Virginia Press, 1908.

LOCHMES, SISTER M. F. *Robert Walsh: His Story.* Washington: The Catholic University Press, 1944.

LOUKES, HAROLD. *The Discovery of Quakerism.* London: George G. Harrap & Co., 1960.

McCLARY, BEN HARRIS. Introduction by. *Letters of Shahcoolen* (1802) by *Benjamin Silliman*. Gainsville, Florida: Scholars' Facsimiles and Reprints, 1962.

MACDONELL, ARTHUR A. *Vedic Index of Names and Subjects.* Varanasi, India: Motilal Banarasidas, 1958.

MAJUMDAR, R., *et al. The History and Culture of the Indian People: The Vedic Age.* I. Bombay: Bharatiya Vidya Bhavan, 1956.

"Manners and Customs of India." *North American Review,* IX (June 1819), 36-58.

MARSHMAN, JOHN C. *The Life and Times of Carey, Marshman, and Ward.* London: Longman, Brown, Green, Longmans, and Roberts, 1859.

MATTHIESSEN, FRANCIS O. *American Renaissance: Art and Expression in the Age of Emerson and Whitman.* New York: Oxford University Press, 1941.

MAYNARD, MILA T. *Walt Whitman: The Poet of the Wider Selfhood.* Chicago: Charles H. Ken and Co., 1903.

MAYO, E. L. "The Influence of Ancient Hindu Thought on Walt Whitman and T. S. Eliot." *The Aryan Path,* XXIX (April 1958), 167-177.

MAX MULLER, FRIEDRICH. *The Vedas.* Calcutta: Susil Gupta Ltd., 1956.

MEESTER, MARIE E., ed. *Oriental Influences in the English Literature of the Nineteenth Century.* Heidelberg: Carl Winters Universtatsbuchhandlung, 1915.

MILLER, PERRY, ed. *The American Transcendentalists: Their Prose and Their Poetry.* New York: Doubleday and Company Inc., 1957.

————. ed. *Consciousness in Concord.* Boston: Houghton, Mifflin and Co., 1958.

————. *The New England Mind: The Seventeenth Century.* Cambridge, Mass.: Harvard University Press, 1963.

MODI, J. J. "Anquetil-Duperron of Pari — India as Seen by Him." *Journal of the Bombay Branch of the Royal Asiatic Society,* XXIV (1917), 313-456.

MONDALE, LESTER. "The Practical Mysticism of Ralph Waldo Emerson," in *Mysticism and the Modern Mind,* ed. by A. P. Steirnotte. New York: Liberal Arts Press, 1960, 43-59.

MONIER-WILLIAMS, SIR MONIER. *Sanskrit-English Dictionary.* Oxford: Oxford University Press, 1960.

————. *Indian Wisdom.* London: Luzac and Co., 1893.

MOORE, ADRIENNE. *Rammohun Roy and America.* Calcutta: Satischandra Chakravarti, 1942.

MOORE, CHARLES A., ed. *Philosophy — East and West.* Princeton: Princeton University Press, 1946.

MOTT, FRANK L. *A History of American Magazines* 1741-1850. Cambridge, Mass., 1939.

MUELDER, WALTER G., and Sears, Laurance. *The Development of American Philosophy: A Book of Readings.* Boston: Houghton, Mifflin and Co., 1940.

NAG, KALIDAS and BURMAN, D., eds. *The English Works of Rajah Rammohun Roy.* Calcutta: Sadharan Brahmo Samaj, 1946.

NAKAMURA, HAJME. *Ways of Thinking of Eastern Peoples: India, China, Tibet, and Japan.* Honolulu: East-West Center Press, 1964.

NYE, RUSSELL. "The Search for the Individual." *Centennial Review,* IV (Summer 1960), 1-20.

OTTO, RUDOLPH. *Mysticism East and West: A Comparative Analysis of the Nature of Mysticism.* New York: The Macmillan Co., 1932.

"Parallels to Hindu and Taoist Thought in Walt Whitman." Unpublished Ph. D. dissertation by Walter K. Malone, Temple University, 1964.

PARRINDER, GEOFFREY. *Upanishads, Gita and Bible: A Comparative Study of Hindu and Christian Scripture.* London: Farber and Farber, 1962.

PAUL, SHERMAN. *The Shores of America: Thoreau's Inward Experience.* Urbana: University of Illinois Press, 1958.

PERRY, BLISS. *Walt Whitman.* New York: Houghton, Mifflin and Co., 1906.

PINTO, VINCENT DE SOLA. "Sir William Jones and English Literature." *Bulletin of Oriental and African Studies,* XI (1946), 685-694.

POCHMANN, HENRY A. *German Culture in America; Philosophical and Literary Influences, 1600-1900.* Madison, Wis., 1953.

————. *New England Transcendentalism and St. Louis Hegelianism: Phases in the History of American Idealism.* Philadelphia: Carl Schurz Foundation, Inc. 1948.

PORTE, JOEL. *Emerson and Thoreau: Transcendentalists in Conflict.* Middletown, Conn.: Wesleyan University Press, 1966.

RADHAKRISHNAN, SARVEPALLI. *The Brahma Sutra: The Philosophy of Spiritual Life.* New York: Harper and Brothers, 1960.

————. Transl. and ed. *The Principal Upanishads.* London: George Allen & Unwin, 1953.

RAJU, P. T. *Indian Idealism and Modern Challenges.* Chandigarh, India: Punjab University Publication Bureau, 1961.

"Rammohun Roy." *Spirit of the Pilgrims,* II (May 1829), 270-278.

"Rammohun Roy." *Unitarian Miscellany and Christian Monitor,* I (January 1822), 74-76.

RANGACHAR, S. *Outlines of the History of Classical Sanskrit Literature.* Mysore: Sanskrit Sahitya Sadana, 1964.

RAPSON, E. J. *Ancient India.* 4th edn. Susil Gupta Ltd., 1960.

"Review of Lord Teignmouth's Life of Sir William Jones." *Christian Observer,* no. 34 (October 1804), 621-629; and no. 35 (November 1804), 693-707.

"Review of 'Professor Everett's Orations.'" *North American Review,* XX (April 1825), 433.

"Review of Roy's 'Defence of Hindu Theism.'" *Analectic Magazine,* XV (February 1820), 129-147.

"Review of 'Select Specimens of the Theatre of the Hindus' by H. H. Wilson." *North American Review,* XXVI (January 1828), 111-126.

REYNOLDS, REGINALD. *The Wisdom of John Woolman.* London: George Allen & Unwin, 1948.

RIEPE, DALE. "Emerson and Indian Philosophy." *Journal of the History of Ideas,* XXVIII (Jan.-Mar. 1967), 115-122.

————. *The Naturalistic Tradition in Indian Thought.* Seattle: Washington University Press, 1961.

RILEY, ISAAC W. *American Thought from Puritanism to Pragmatism and Beyond.* New York: Peter Smith, 1941.

SCHLEGEL, FREDERICK. *Lectures on the History of Literature, Ancient and Modern.* London: H. G. Bohn, 1859.

SCHNEIDER, HERBERT W. *A History of American Philosophy.* New York: Columbia University Press, 1946.

SCHWEITZER, ALBERT. *Indian Thought and Its Development.* Translated by Mrs. Charles E. B. Russell. London: The Beacon Press, 1960.

SINGH, IQBAL. *Rammohun Roy: A Biographical Inquiry into the Making of Modern India.* 2 vols. Bombay: Asia Publishing House, 1958.

SMITHLINE, ARNOLD. *Natural Religion in American Literature.* New Haven, Conn.: College and University Press, 1966.

SOWERBY, E. MILLICENT, (comp.) *Catalogue of the Library of Thomas Jefferson.* 6 vols. Washington: Library of Congress, 1959.

SRIKHANDE, V. B. "The Nature of Self," in *Recent Indian Philosophy.* Edited by Kalidas Bhattacharya. Calcutta: Progressive Publishers, 1963.

STEIN, WILLIAM B., *et al.* "Emerson's 'Brahma.'" *Explicator* (December 1961), Item 29.

————. *Two Brahman Sources of Emerson and Thoreau.* Gainsville, Fla.: Scholars' Facsimile and Reprints, 1967.

STACE, W. T. *Mysticism and Philosophy.* Philadelphia: J. B. Lippincott, 1960.

STEWART, RANDALL. "A Doctrine of Man." *Mississippi Quarterly,* XII (Winter 1959), 4-9.

STOVALL, FLOYD. *American Idealism.* Norman: University of Oklahoma Press, 1943.

STRAUCH, CARL F. "Emerson as Literary Middleman." *Emerson Society Quarterly* (1960 II Quarter), 2-9.

The Travels of ..., William Bartram. Edited by Francis Harper, New Haven: Yale University Press, 1958.

THOREAU, HENRY D. *A Week on Concord and Merrimack Rivers.* Boston and New York: Houghton, Mifflin and Co., 1906.

————. *The Collected Poems of ....* Edited by Carl Bode. Chicago: Packard and Co., 1943.

————. *The Correspondence of ....* Edited by Walter Harding and Carl Bode. New York: New York University Press, 1958.

————. *The Writings of* . . . . 20 vols. Boston and New York: Houghton, Mifflin ana Co., 1906.

TENDULKAR, D. G. "The Influence of Thoreau's Civil Disobedience on Gandhi's *Satyagraha.*" *New England Quarterly,* XXIX (December 1956), 7-8.

TOLLES, FREDERICK B. "Emerson and Quakerism." *American Literature,* X (May 1938), 142-162.

TUDOR, WILLIAM. "Theology of the Hindoos, as Taught by Ram Mohan Roy." *North American Review,* VI (March 1818), 386-393.

VAJDA, GEORGE. "The Dialectics of the Talmud and the Kabbalah." *Diogenes* (Fall 1967), 63-79.

VAN DOREN, MARK, ed. *The Travels of William Bartram.* New York: Dover Publications, 1928.

Vedanta Dictionary. Compiled by Ernest Wood. New York: Philosophical Library, 1964.

VOGEL, STANLEY M. *German Literary Influences on the American Transcendentalists.* New Haven: Yale University Press, 1955.

WADE, MASON. *Margaret Fuller: Whetstone of Genius.* New York: The Viking Press, 1940.

Walt Whitman: Leaves of Grass and Selected Prose. Edited by Sculley Bradley. New York: Holt, Rinehart and Winston, 1960.

Walt Whitman's Leaves of Grass: The First (1855) *Edition.* Introduction by Malcolm Cowley. New York: The Viking Press, 1959.

Walt Whitman: The Correspondence (1842-1867). Edited by Edwin E. Miller, I. New York: New York University Press, 1961.

Walt Whitman: The Early Poems and the Fiction. Edited by Thomas L. Brasher. New York: New York University Press, 1963.

Walt Whitman: Prose Works 1892. Edited by Floyd Stovall, I. New York: New York University Press, 1963. This and the two preceding entries are part of *The Collected Works of Walt Whitman* so far under the general editorship of Gay W. Allen and Sculley Bradley.

WELLEK, RENE. "Emerson and German Philosophy." *New England Quarterly,* XVI (March 1943), 41-62.

WELLS, RONALD V. *Three Christian Transcendentalists: James Marsh, Caleb Sprague Henry, Frederic Hedge.* New York: Columbia University Press, 1943.

WERNER, W. L. "Whitman's ' The Mystic Trumpeteer:' An Autobiography." *American Literature,* VII (January 1936), 455-458.

WHITTIER, JOHN G., ed. *The Journal of John Woolman.* Boston: Houghton, Mifflin and Co., 1871.

WISCHER, STEPHEN E. *Freedom and Fate: An Inner Life of Waldo Emerson.* Philadelphia: University of Pennsylvania Press, 1953.

WILLIAMS, GEORGE W. Compiler. *Catalogue of the Library of the Reverend James Warley Miles.* Reprinted from the surviving copy of the Charleston edition of 1854. Charleston, S. C.: University of Virginia Press, 1955.

WOOD, JAMES. *Magazines in the United States.* New York: The Ronald Press, 1949.

WOODCOCK, GEORGE. *The Greeks in India.* London: Faber and Faber, 1966, 149-163.

WOOLMAN, JOHN. *The Journal of* .... Edited by John G. Whittier. Boston: Houghton, Mifflin and Co., 1871.

WYMAN, MARY A. "Goethe, Emerson and Whitehead on God in the World," in *The Lure for Feeling in the Creative Process.* New York: Philosophical Library, 1960, 43-103.

ZAEHNER, R. C. *Mysticism, Sacred and Profane: An Inquiry into Some Varieties of Experience.* Oxford: Clarendon Press, 1957.

ZIMMER, HEINRICH. *Myths and Symbols in Indian Art and Civilization.* Edited by Joseph Campbell. New York: Harper Torch Books, 1962.

————. *Philosophies of India.* Edited by Joseph Campbell. New York: Princeton University Press, 1967.

INDEX

Adam, William, 78
advaita, 65, 68, 87
American Baptist Magazine, 91
American Quarterly Review, 43, 110
American transcendentalism, 9
Analytic Magazine, 90
Asia, 5, 7
Asiatick Miscellany, 49, 50, 51, 57, 84, 97, 112
Asiatick Researches, 53, 54, 55, 57, 71, 72, 82, 83, 84, 85, 88, 92, 113, 115
Ātman, 19, 20, 21, 22, 24, 31, 65
Avidya, 22

Bacon, Thomas, 119
Bartram, William, 33-36
Bhagavad-Gita, 13-14, 17, 18, 27, 47, 71, 116
Bhakti, 24
Boston Magazine, 80
Brahma, 30
Brahman, 9, 18-20, 21, 22, 24, 29, 31, 65, 69, 83, 85, 104
Brahmin, 7-9
brahminism, 8, 9
Brāhmaṇa, 8, 9, 64
Buddhism, 9

Calcott, Lady Maria, 78-79, 118
"Camdeo," 48, 50, 59, 84
Carey, William, 74-75, 116
Carpenter, Frederic I., 3-10
Caunter, Hobart, 118
Channing, Edward T., 86
Chari, V. K., 113
Christianity, 4, 24, 25
Christian Register, 90

Christy, Arthur, 9-12
Colebrooke, Henry T., 72-73, 92, 114, 115
Commercial Advertiser, 82, 83
compassion, 31, 33
Cowley, Malcolm, 14
"Curse of Kehama," 95

Degerando, Joseph M., 65, 66, 91, 99, 102, 119
Dial, 1, 93, 101, 103, 104, 105, 106
Dubois, Abbé, J. A., 67-71, 86, 92, 103, 120
Duperron, Anquetil, 61-68, 71, 119

Edinburgh Review, 98, 101
Edwards, Jonathan, 25-26
Emanation, 26, 65, 66, 76
Emerson and Asia, 3-10
Emerald, 89
Emerson, Ralph W., 1, 2-10, 15, 66, 74, 94, 95-103, 105
Everett, Edward, 85, 92

Fate, 6-7, 22
Fox, George, 32
Franklin, Benjamin, 41, 42, 45, 46, 47, 58, 59
Frothingham, Octavus B., VIII

Gita Govinda, 27, 54, 55, 83, 120
Goren, Leyla, 8

Heber, Bishop Reginold, 118
Hindus, Hindoos, 6, 75, 89, 101, 102, 114, 115, 117

Harivansa, 11, 70
Hitopadesa, 31, 49, 53, 71, 104, 114, 115, 116

Identity, 21
"Indian Superstition," 95
Indo-Germanic family of languages, 52
Immanence, 21, 31, 34, 36, 66

Jefferson, Thomas, 40, 41, 45, 55, 59, 110, 112
Jesus, 24, 25
Jones, Sir William, 36, 37-57, 92, 108-114

Kabbalah, 24
Karma, 6, 22

Langlois, Alexander, 70, 71, 120
Lassen, Christian, 120
Leaves of Grass, 12-14, 104
Letters of Shahcoolen, 51, 82, 83, 84, 92
Literary Miscellany, 85

Manava-Dharma-Sastra, 48, 49, 50, 53
Manu, 1, 17, 85, 96, 100, 102, 104
Marsh, James, 91
Marshman, Joshua, 75, 79
Māya, 11, 20, 21, 22, 65, 69, 73, 83, 84, 87, 88, 90
Megasthanes, 2
Miller, Perry, 10, 26, 102
Monthly Register, 81, 82
Mott, Frank L., 81
Murray, Hugh, 118
Museum of Foreign Literature and Science, 43, 110

Nakamura, Hajme, 5

"Narayena," 50-51, 59, 66, 97
New York Review and Athenaeum Magazine, 90
North American Review, 86, 88, 89

Ode in Imitation of Alcaeus, 42, 43, 58, 110
Ordinances of Manu, 48, 53, 55, 56, 57, 100 114
Orient, 3, 5, 12
Orient in American Transcendentalism, The, 9-13
Original Sin, 25
Oupnek'hat, 62, 63, 65, 66, 91, 99, 119

Panini, 4, 52, 72
Plato, 2, 45
Puritanism, 24

Quaker, 25, 30, 31, 32
Quarterly Rerview, 94, 101

Ritter, Heinrich, 117
Rixner, Thaddae A., 65
Roy, Rammohan, 75, 77, 78, 80, 89, 90, 91, 92, 118

Sakuntala, 55, 56, 59, 113
Schweitzer, Albert, 15
Southey, Robert, 94, 95, 96
Stiles, Dr. Ezra, 76

Taylor, Edward, 26-30
Terry, Edward, Chaplain to Sir Thomas Rowe, 118
Thoreau, Henry D., 1, 15, 34, 102-103
Transcendentalism, 3, 9, 10
Tudor, William, 89, 92

Upanisads, 6, 7, 8, 9, 16, 17, 18, 64, 65, 72

Vedanta, 6, 15, 16, 22, 23, 37, 64, 65, 72, 73, 75, 77, 91, 106
Vedantic philosophy, 1, 15-17, 61, 67, 71, 76, 78, 79, 80, 81, 84, 87, 88, 89, 90, 91, 92, 97, 98, 99, 100, 104, 105, 107
Vedic literature, 1, 17, 18, 61, 67, 70, 71, 73, 76, 78, 79, 80, 81, 84, 92, 93, 98, 99, 100, 102, 104, 105, 106, 107

Vedas, 64, 70, 72, 75, 85, 89, 90, 100, 102, 115, 118
Vishnu Purana, 74, 115

Wagner, Udolph, 117
Ward, William, 75, 76, 98, 117
Whitman, Walt, 12-15, 104, 105
Wilkins, Charles, 13, 47, 116
Wilson, Horace H., 73, 115, 116
Woolman, John, 31, 32
Works of the British Poets, 43, 84, 110